The Origins
and Evolution
of the Arab-Zionist
Conflict

The Origins
and Evolution
of the Arab-Zionist
Conflict

MICHAEL J. COHEN

UNIVERSITY OF CALIFORNIA PRESS
BERKELEY / LOS ANGELES / LONDON

University of California Press
Berkeley and Los Angeles, California

University of California Press, Ltd.
London, England

© 1987 by
The Regents of the University of California

Library of Congress Cataloging-in-Publication Data
Cohen, Michael Joseph, 1940–
  The origins and evolution of the Arab-Zionist
conflict.
  Bibliography: p.
  Includes index.
  1. Jewish-Arab relations—1917–1949.   2. Palestine—
History—1917–1948.   I. Title.
DS119.7.C633   1987   956'.03   86–16060
ISBN 0–520–05821–6 (alk. paper)

Printed in the United States of America
1 2 3 4 5 6 7 8 9

For Ilan and Natalie

Contents

List of Maps

List of Documents

Preface

From gestation to publication is sometimes a long process. This book originated in four lectures I gave in 1980 when I was Visiting Professor with the Cooperative Program in Judaic Studies at Duke University and the University of North Carolina, Chapel Hill. The manuscript was completed at the University of British Columbia, Vancouver, B.C., in 1985. I extend my thanks and deep appreciation to these institutions, and I am particularly grateful for the generosity of the History Department at the University of British Columbia.

My purpose here is to present the student, or indeed the educated general reader, with an analytical introduction to the Arab-Israeli conflict, as well as some guide to the literature thereon. My justification for writing yet another book on this issue is, first, that most of the books covering the Palestine mandate are lengthy textbooks that at times make for heavy reading and, next, that most were written at least fifteen to twenty years ago and now need updating.

I am not seeking to add yet another textbook to the pile, and I shall limit myself to four specific questions: Why, and under what circumstances, did the British government make certain commitments to the Arabs and the Jews during World War I? What was the respective nature of those commitments? What were the fundamental contradictions and problems that doomed the Palestine mandate from its inception? And, fourth, what led Britain to give up the mandate after World War II and the Arabs and Jews to engage in their first war?

My book should therefore be regarded as a guide for students of the Middle East and for the intelligent nonspecialist. I hope that it will clarify some controversies that do not always receive full or objective treatment in lengthier texts. My goal has been not so much to unravel fresh evidence (although my own research has contributed to the final two chapters), as to present a dispassionate, intelligible analysis of the evidence available in the 1980s. It is to be hoped that students will find this a simple, though not simplistic, overview of a complex subject, to be used prior to their delving into the heavier tomes of academic, and some not-so-academic, research. Some of the basic policy documents, mainly official statements of British policy, have been included in a section following the text.

All unpublished Crown copyright material from the Public Record Office appears by permission of the Controller of HM Stationery Office.

CHAPTER ONE

Arab Nationalism and British Promises of Independence During World War I

Intellectual and Political Developments Before 1914

At the end of the eighteenth century the greater part of the Middle East formed part of the Ottoman empire. The overwhelming majority of its inhabitants were Muslims who since the conquest of the area by the Ottomans in the sixteenth century had given their political allegiance to the Ottoman sultan. The sultan also laid claim to the caliphate, but by the questionable right of conquest rather than by the traditional right of inheritance by descent from the family, or tribe, of the prophet Muhammad. During the four centuries of Ottoman rule, Islam declined from the intellectual and cultural zenith it had reached in the Middle Ages. In the words of Bernard Lewis:

> The Ottoman Empire was the last and the most enduring of the great Islamic universal empires. . . . Within it, the basic loyalty of Muslims was to Islam, to the Islamic Empire that was its political embodiment, and to the dynasty, legitimized by time and acceptance, that ruled over it. . . . Until the impact of European political ideas, the Arab subjects of the Ottoman Em-

pire, though well aware of their separate linguistic and cultural identity and of the historic memories attached to them, had no conception of a separate Arab state, and no serious desire to part from the Turks. Certainly, they did not question the fact that the Sultans happened to be Turkish. On the contrary, they would have found it odd had they been anything else. So alien was the idea of the territorial nation state that Arabic had no word for Arabia, while Turkish, until modern times, lacked a word for Turkey.[1]

The conquest of Egypt by Napoleon in 1798 (a "sideshow" in his revolutionary wars against Britain) sent out traumatic shock waves among the Muslims living in the Middle East. What was the secret behind the West's apparent superiority? What had been responsible for Islam's decline into apathetic indifference? Could Islam now digest the science, culture, and values of the West without fatally compromising its own divinely ordered world? Above all, how could Islam's self-image of preordained superiority be squared with the demonstrable superiority of the West? These were the questions that plagued intellectuals in the East, questions that had to be resolved before traditional Muslim society could ever agree that it had anything at all to learn from the West.

The meeting of Islamic traditional society with Western secular nationalism provoked spiritual and political tensions. It inaugurated an irreversible process, as described in the following passage written by Shafik Gorbal, one of Egypt's leading historians:

The period of a hundred and fifty years which began with the French invasion of Egypt in 1213 (A.D. 1798)

1. Bernard Lewis, *The Middle East and the West* (Bloomington, Ind., 1964), pp. 72–73.

witnessed the merging of our Islamic society into the world society of the present era. We, the members of the Islamic society, have not been fully aware of all the implications of the events of this period. . . . The influence has been so great that even when the Islamic people have regained their political independence they have found that a return to the traditional way of life was not possible—even if it were desirable. It needs to be emphasized that such a return is not deemed desirable even when lip-service is paid to the glorious traditions of the past.[2]

The peoples of the Middle East were not homogeneous. Only in the twentieth century, with the advent of indigenous nationalism, did they begin to take on the common identity of "Arabs." Even so, they were divided into an overwhelming majority of Muslims and a Christian minority. The Muslims themselves were divided into an orthodox Sunni majority and a Shia minority concentrated in Iraq and Persia. Muslim attitudes differed from Christian, Syrian from Egyptian.

A Muslim reform movement tried to bridge the gap between Islamic and Western culture by claiming the right to reinterpret Islamic doctrine in the spirit of true Islam as taught by the prophet Muhammad and the community of Elders (al-Salaf, the pious forerunners). Muhammad Abduh (1849–1905), the greatest of the Islamic reformers, claimed that there could be no intrinsic conflict between the Koran and modern science and that any apparent contradictions were the result of a misunderstanding of one or the other. Abduh tried to put his teachings into effect when he served as mufti of Egypt at the end of the nineteenth

2. Quoted in Kenneth W. Morgan, ed., *Islam: The Straight Path* (New York, 1958), p. 78.

century. For example, he overruled Islamic proscriptions of usury and allowed lending at interest, a prerequisite of modern capitalist investment.

But there were obvious dangers in opening up to modern interpretation the orthodox doctrines as laid down by the great theologians of the third and fourth Islamic centuries. Abduh himself was subject to fierce attack from conservatives, and when reform developed into secularism and agnosticism, Abduh's disciple, Rashid Rida (1865–1935), the last of the reformers, reverted back to a conservative, orthodox Islam.

In contrast, the Christian Arabs had maintained both religious and worldly (trade) contacts with the West since the Middle Ages. Being themselves highly vulnerable in a society predicated on Islamic hierarchy, the Christians were only too ready to adopt Western values such as liberalism and separation of church and state. It is therefore no coincidence that the center of the intellectual and cultural renaissance was in Lebanon, where Christians such as Butrus Bustani (1819–1883) embarked upon the translation of the great literary masterpieces of the West into Arabic. During the 1870s groups calling themselves the "Young Christians" worked clandestinely for Syrian territorial autonomy, with the goal of a secular society that would avert a repetition of the religious wars that had racked Lebanon in the 1860s. But the Muslims would not cooperate in working toward a Syrian secular state. The Ottoman regime persecuted and suppressed those working for constitutional reform of any kind. Many Christian intellectuals fled Lebanon for the more progressive clime of British-ruled Egypt. There they established the great publishing houses and newspapers that adorn Egypt to this day.

These intellectual stirrings were stifled and blocked

somewhat during the last quarter of the nineteenth century, when Western imperialism made its most pronounced military drive into the region. Tunisia, Egypt, Morocco, and Libya were conquered and occupied by France, Britain, and Italy at the end of the nineteenth and the beginning of the twentieth centuries. Muslim conservatives asserted that Western reforms were but a trap, designed to lay Islam open to conquest by the imperialists. The conservatives warned that the attempt to adopt Western values would destroy the pristine purity of Islam, and with it the secret of Muslim superiority. Their course must be to return to Islam as conceived by the Prophet, under whom they had made their greatest advances.

Complementing this trend was the Pan-Islamic movement, whose political head was the sultan-caliph, who made political use of the ideology supplied by Jamal al-Din al-Afghani (1839–1897), a political agitator who had collaborated with Abduh to promote a local nationalist movement in Egypt earlier on. For al-Afghani the threat of Western imperialism was apparently more immediate than that of Ottoman backwardness. Muslims as far afield as India and Afghanistan were incited to rebel against the imperialist powers. For the Ottoman sultan the call to a united crusade against imperialism served to distract his subjects from their various ethnic struggles for greater local autonomy, which would inevitably have loosened the Ottoman grip on the peripheral provinces.

The Pan-Islamic movement, combined with a fair measure of suppression and persecution within the empire, served to maintain Arab fidelity to the sultan-caliph. At the turn of the nineteenth century a few intellectuals began to urge Arab secession from the empire, blaming the Ottomans for the trough in which Islam then found itself. They pointed to the evident fact that Islam had achieved its greatest successes prior to the Ottoman conquest in the sixteenth century, and some went so far as to claim the existence of an Arab nation prior even to the advent of the Prophet. They claimed that Islam had been diluted with alien innovations and that only in the remote Arabian peninsula had something of the original pure religion been preserved.

The case of the Arabs against the Turks was put in a radical fashion by Abd al-Rahman al-Kawakibi (1849–1902), who left his native Aleppo for Egypt in 1898 in obscure circumstances and whose writings seem to have been unacknowledged cribs or adaptations of Western orientalists. He claimed that the current stagnation of Islam was the result both of Ottoman tyranny and of the absence of racial and linguistic bonds among Muslims. Partly for this reason, the Ottoman empire must be considered unfit to preserve Islam, whose regeneration should be the work of the Arabs. The latter should supply a caliph, who would be descended from the Prophet's own tribe, that of Quraysh. This caliph would reside at Mecca in Arabia and, contrary to traditional notions, would exercise no political power. He would be left with merely religious authority, like an Islamic pope, a symbol of Islamic unity. As the first to declare himself unambiguously against the Turks, al-Kawakibi may be considered the "first true intellectual precursor of modern secular Pan-Arabism." In addition, "by launching, in Arabic, the idea of a merely spiritual caliphate he took the first step toward a purely secular politics . . . an essential prerequisite of nationalism."[3]

3. Sylvia G. Haim, *Arab Nationalism: An Anthology* (Berkeley and Los Angeles, 1962), p. 27.

But nascent Arab nationalism at the beginning of the twentieth century was confined to a small group of intellectuals. The most significant claims on the loyalty of the masses were those of the family, village, and sultan-caliph. In 1908 the Ottoman sultan was deposed by the Committee of Union and Progress (CUP), a radical reform group composed mainly of intellectuals and officers. The CUP announced the dawn of a new liberal era and reopened the parliament, which had been adjourned indefinitely over thirty years before, after a brief life span of one year. But the CUP notion of constitutional reform did not coincide with that of its subject peoples. Internal and external crises buffeted the new regime. There was revolution and counterrevolution at home, and loss of territory abroad (most of Turkey's remaining European territory was surrendered during the Balkan Wars of 1912–1913, and Libya was ceded to the Italians in 1913). The consequence was a retreat from liberalism to conservative nationalism at home. In place of Pan-Islam the Turks adopted its antithesis, Pan-Turanism, an extreme form of Turkish nationalism that looked back to, and transformed into a cult, the Turks' legendary origins in Turan in eastern Asia.

The Arabs in the Ottoman empire had helped the CUP into power (as indeed had the Jews), believing that the CUP's promises of reform would include greater civil rights and autonomy for them, too. But where Pan-Islam had united all Islam under a single banner, Pan-Turanism threatened to arouse provincial nationalisms by attempting to impose Turkish culture down to the local level.

In the Arab provinces, especially in Egypt and in Syria, small groups began to organize, with programs demanding greater local autonomy. One group based in Cairo actually called itself the Ottoman Decentralization party, and even enjoyed the support of some Turkish liberals. Other groups, such as al-ʿAhd (the Covenant Society, formed primarily by army officers in 1914) and al-Fatah (The Young Arab, formed by students in 1911), had to meet in secret, and tried, not always with success, to keep one step ahead of the Turkish secret police. As its name indicates, the Ottoman Decentralization party asked for greater use of Arabic and more jobs for Arabs in the Arabic provinces. The secret societies conceived a political solution modeled on the Austro-Hungarian empire, a model soon to suffer its final demise in World War I. These Arabs proposed a Turco-Arab dual monarchy that, while permitting the expression of Arab national rights, would preserve central Turkish control over such "federal" matters as communications, the army, and foreign affairs.

The final initiative of these groups was the convening of a conference in Paris in July 1913 to publicize their demands in the West and, it was hoped, mobilize diplomatic pressure to force the Turks to accede to them. After failing to stop the conference, the Turks beat a tactical retreat and agreed to negotiate the Arabs' demands. But having once secured the safe adjournment of the Paris conference, the Turks made symbolic concessions that were a hollow mockery of Arab demands. The secret societies were now convinced that no constitutional progress was to be hoped for from the autocratic Turkish regime.

Thus on the eve of World War I the initial stirrings of the Arab national movement had come to a halt. Frustrated in its efforts to wring even minor concessions from the Turks, a small minority of articulate intellectuals and army officers was moving gradually toward the idea of complete secession. However, this small group was hardly ready or able to challenge the Turkish regime, at least not without a foreign patron, which as yet it lacked. The vast majority of the Arab world adhered to the new Turkish regime, which had had the political sagacity to retain the institution of the caliphate as a symbol of Muslim unity. For this overwhelming majority of the faithful the very concept of an Arab alliance with an alien, Christian nation against the Muslim caliph would raise acute problems of religious identity.

Husayn and the Arab National Movement

In 1914, as the clouds of World War I gathered on the horizon, little movement was visible on the surface in the Middle East, where it seemed that Turkish rule might hold sway indefinitely. Although Zionist settlement in the Holy Land had aroused some Arab opposition, there was as yet no territorial unit by the name of Palestine and no Palestinian problem, and, as we shall see, the Zionist movement itself was in political limbo. For both Arabs and Jews World War I would offer unique political opportunities. Each movement had run into insuperable difficulties with the Turks, but by the close of the Great War Britain would replace Turkey as the political suzerain of the Middle East.

The sharif Husayn was a scion of the Hashemite family, descended from the Prophet and traditional guardians of Islam's most holy sites, Mecca and Medina, in the Arabian province of Hijaz. Husayn had been detained under house arrest in Constantinople for many years by the last sultan, Abdülhamid II, who had feared a movement to promote Husayn as Arab caliph. In 1908 the CUP had allowed Husayn to return to the Hijaz, hoping that he would rally the peninsular Arabs to the new regime.

But Husayn harbored his own dynastic ambitions in the Hijaz and did not settle down to the role of quiescent vassal. The Hashemites had played no part in the intellectual and national renaissance of the nineteenth and early twentieth centuries, but in 1914, with the Arab secret societies at a dead end, the Hashemites, albeit with their own local interests at heart, would forge the vital link between the Arabs and the West, a link that would provide the key to the fulfillment of Arab aspirations.

Following the example set by Muhammad Ali in Egypt, Husayn sought to establish the Hashemite dynasty as independent sovereigns in the Hijaz. After Husayn's return in 1908, relations with the local Turkish governor (*wali*) deteriorated rapidly. When the Turks sent a new, young, and vigorous governor, Husayn feared they intended to tighten their grip, if not actually to depose him. Expecting an imminent clash, Husayn dispatched his son 'Abdallah (later to be the ruler of Transjordan, 1921–1952) on a mission to Cairo.

At Cairo 'Abdallah asked the British representative, Lord Kitchener, if the British would adopt a sympathetic attitude to the Hashemites if they rebelled against the Turks. The British were interested in the stability of the Hijaz, the site of the annual Islamic pilgrimage, which many of Britain's Muslim subjects made. The Hijaz was also of great strategic importance, lying near the egress of the Suez Canal. But in early 1914 the British still adhered rigidly to their "Eastern Policy," which since the 1840s had propped up the ailing Ottoman empire against foreign (mainly Russian) encroachment. Britain had as yet no incentive for supporting one of the Turks' vassals in a conflict with his sovereign.

'Abdallah continued by sea from Cairo to Constantinople, where he paid homage to his Turkish overlord. Upon his return to Cairo in April 1914 he again pressed the British. This time he was received by the oriental secretary, Ronald Storrs, who was destined to play a central role in the correspondence with the sharif. Storrs again made it quite clear that the British could give no aid whatever to the Hashemites should they become involved in a conflict with the Turks. The British as yet attributed little significance to the Arab national movement, for which, moreover, they had little political use. Further, it must be emphasized again that 'Abdallah was not making any demands on behalf of the Arabs in general, but specifically on behalf of his family's interest in the Hijaz.

The British attitude toward the Arabs would change as Britain's military fortunes in the Near East deteriorated during the course of 1915. Once the Turks entered the war on the German side in late October 1914, Lord Kitchener (transferred from Cairo to London in 1914 to become secretary of state for war) perceived that the Hashemites might help the British war effort. Kitchener had served for many years with the British army in India, and he was now anxious about the continued loyalty of India's Muslims in Britain's impending conflict with the Turks. India provided the bulk of Britain's land armies.[4] How would Muslim soldiers react if the Turkish caliph called for a jihad (holy war) against the Allies? If Britain could promote the transfer of the caliphate to an Arab candidate beholden to them, obvious advantages would accrue, not only in India but also in the Middle East itself, soon to become a major theater of war.

On 31 October 1914 Kitchener asked Storrs to convey to Husayn a message intimating that if the Arabs helped

4. See John Darwin, *Britain, Egypt, and the Middle East: Imperial Policy in the Aftermath of War, 1918–1922* (London, 1981), p. 12.

the Allied cause in the war, then perhaps "an Arab of the true race will assume the Caliphate at Mecca or Medina." Some commentators have claimed that Kitchener did not fully grasp the significance of his offer, that he understood the caliphate to be something akin to an Islamic papacy— that is to say, with spiritual authority only.[5] As we have seen, there were some, such as al-Kawakibi, who indeed wanted to return the caliphate to the Hijaz and restrict the caliph's temporal authority to that province alone. Whatever the case, Husayn himself interpreted Kitchener's hint about the caliphate to imply its full military and political connotations as well. In this way Kitchener's initiative was instrumental in transforming Husayn's limited political ambition in the Hijaz into a wider dream of Hashemite suzerainty over the far greater regions of the Arab-populated Middle East.

But Husayn was still not quite ready to commit himself to the Allied cause, fearing Turkish reprisals, against which the British were as yet unable to shield him. Further, apart from his own desert tribesmen, mounted on camels, Husayn had no military forces to offer the Allies or to use in making good his territorial claims. His next step was to establish contact with the Arab secret societies, who had both a political program and the trained officers who might provide a military option.

In March 1915 Husayn's third son, Faysal, set off to pay homage in Constantinople, taking the overland route via Damascus, cradle of the Arab nationalist movement. There he met with and joined the secret societies al-Fatah and al-ʿAhd. Faysal was greatly impressed with the organiza-

5. Elie Kedourie, *England and the Middle East* (London, 1956), pp. 52–53.

tion of al-ʿAhd, whose leaders claimed they were able to provoke a revolt of the Arab divisions in the Turkish army at will. The Ottoman divisions then stationed in Syria were overwhelmingly Arab, and many of their officers were members of al-ʿAhd.

Faysal proceeded on to Constantinople, where he was treated with unusual deference and consideration. The Turks stated that the remedy to the situation in the Hijaz lay in Husayn's own hands. If only he would declare himself openly in favor of the jihad, he might count on the satisfaction of his demands.

Faysal stopped off once more in Damascus at the end of May on his way back home. In his absence the leaders of al-Fatah and al-ʿAhd had drawn up a protocol defining the conditions under which the Arab leaders would be prepared to cooperate with Britain against Turkey. The program, now called the Damascus Protocol, asked for British recognition of Arab independence within borders that included the countries known today as Lebanon, Syria, Jordan, Iraq, Saudi Arabia, and Israel. The protocol, which offered a defensive alliance between Britain and the future independent Arab state, was taken by Faysal to Mecca, where it was adopted as the program of the Hashemites. Faysal himself was profoundly suspicious of the Allies' intentions, and he expressed doubts as to the prospects of their accepting the Arabs' conditions. But he agreed that the protocol was a minimum on which a call to revolt might be justified and undertook to secure his father's approval. Six of the secret society leaders thereupon pledged themselves to recognize the sharif as spokesman of the Arab race and promised that in the event the Hashemites secured an agreement with Great Britain on the basis of the Damascus Protocol, the Arab divisions in Syria would rise to a man.[6] The Damascus Protocol formed the basis of Husayn's first letter in what became known as the Husayn-McMahon correspondence, an exchange since described as "at once deliberately vague and unwittingly obscure."

The Husayn-McMahon Correspondence, July 1915–January 1916

On 14 July 1915, shortly after Faysal's return to Mecca, Husayn sent off his first letter to the new British high commissioner for Egypt, Sir Henry McMahon. As noted above, the letter included the territorial demands of the Damascus Protocol and sought British agreement to the proclamation of an Arab caliphate for Islam. The latter demand was highly irregular; no caliph had ever sought or required the sanction of a Western, Christian power. Husayn was evidently reminding the British of Kitchener's hint of the previous October, perhaps as a test of British seriousness.

When the Middle East became a theater of war, Cairo became the nerve center of the British civilian and military administrations in the region. In July 1915, with an Indian army advancing into Mesopotamia and the fate of the Dardanelles expedition still in the balance, the Cairo officials did not regard the time as ripe for such far-reaching concessions to the Arabs, who had as yet to demonstrate their concrete value to the Allied cause. On the contrary, the fact that Arab soldiers were at that juncture fighting with the Turks against the British side in Mesopotamia made Husayn's demands seem downright pretentious. Thus Husayn's overture was rebuffed as being premature and a waste of time, all the more so "as a party of Arabs inhabiting those very regions have, to our amazement and sorrow, over-

6. George Antonius, *The Arab Awakening* (London, 1938), p. 158.

looked and neglected this invaluable and incomparable opportunity; and, instead of coming to our aid, have lent their assistance to the Germans and the Turks."

The Arabs had perhaps hoped for too much from Kitchener. He was a legendary figure in the East, and the Arabs did not then appreciate the limits of an individual minister's authority in a constitutional democracy. McMahon's rebuff was thus all the more difficult to digest. In his next letter Husayn stressed that he was pursuing not merely his own personal ambition but also the aspirations of the entire Arab nation, whose representative he was.

The British were not impressed by Husayn's rhetoric. But the deteriorating fortunes of the British war effort in the Near East, particularly in the Dardanelles campaign, provided the critical catalyst that brought about a change of heart in Cairo.

As the war on the Western Front bogged down in the trenches, a fierce debate ensued between those who called themselves "Easterners" (mainly politicians) and the "Westerners" (the military). The "Easterners" claimed that trench warfare was achieving nothing but the attrition of the flower of British youth; what was needed, they asserted, was a flanking campaign in the East that would take the Turks out of the war and open up further alternatives for getting at the Germans. The "Westerners" retorted with orthodox military doctrine that all forces must be concentrated and thrown against the main concentration of German military might, that only in this way could they hope to break the enemy. Winston Churchill, first lord of the Admiralty at the beginning of the war, was the forceful leader of the "Easterners" and convinced the cabinet to attempt to force the Dardanelles and capture Constantinople.

Kitchener, who himself favored landings in the Alexandretta (now Iskenderun) area in order to cut off the Turkish army from its home bases, was slow to offer the army's support for the campaign, which thus began in February 1915 as a purely naval effort to force the strait. The naval attack broke up and retreated after it lost several ships in the narrow portion of the strait. It was now agreed to support the naval forces with troop landings on the Gallipoli Peninsula in order to neutralize the heavy guns sited along its high shores. But the element of surprise had been lost, and the Turks, ably guided by the Germans, had ample time to strengthen their defenses. Turkish forces, led by a brilliant young cavalry officer, Mustafa Kemal Pasha (who subsequently, as Kemal Atatürk, founded and became the first president of modern Turkey), were able during the summer to repel successive Allied landings.

The last of the major Allied assaults on the Gallipoli Peninsula, at Suvla Bay, was repelled in August; it was then just a matter of time before the British conceded failure and attempted to withdraw their forces. It was during this period that Husayn's second letter, dated 9 September, was received. McMahon himself testified later that the British commander at the strait had at that time appealed to Cairo in desperation, urging some initiative to bring about the withdrawal of the Arab forces then fighting alongside the Turks at the strait (the Arab divisions had been transferred there from Syria, where the Turks had suspected and feared an Arab revolt).

One additional factor tipped the scales. In September a Kurdish soldier named al-Faruqi, who had been fighting at the strait, defected to the British side while on a routine mission across the lines to exchange dead and wounded. Faruqi was brought to Cairo for interrogation by British Intelligence. Historians are for once unanimous in their agreement that Faruqi's testimony in Cairo was decisive in persuading British officials there to respond positively to Husayn's demands. Large areas of disagreement remain, however, over Faruqi's veracity and the reliability of his evidence.

Faruqi told his interrogators that the Arab nationalist movement was organized in numerous cells across the Arab world, with coffers containing thousands of pounds in membership fees. He warned that the Arabs were being pressed to ally themselves with the Germans and that although the Arabs would prefer the Allies, they would be left with no choice but to side with the Germans if they did not receive some positive response to Husayn's overtures soon.

The Cairo officials believed that matters had come to a head and that the British must choose a successor to the Turks in the Middle East, one through whom they would be able to continue to exercise influence in the area. And what better candidates than the Hashemites, with whom they had longstanding contacts and who enjoyed the status of spiritual leaders in the Arab world? Faruqi thus found it easy to convince the Arab experts at Cairo in September 1915—he was speaking to the converted. British Intelligence made no serious effort to check his evidence. Had they done so, they would have discovered that the Arab nationalist movement in Syria had already been emasculated by the Turks and that all regular Arab units serving with the Turkish armies had been transferred to other fronts. It would have then been apparent that all hopes of a revolt by the Arab divisions, upon which the proposed alliance was still predicated, had been dashed. When the Arab revolt did eventually materialize in June 1916, it was based on the guerrilla activities of Hashemite Bedouins, habituated to tribal, desert warfare.

Cairo's sponsorship of the Hashemites would, moreover, soon bring about a conflict in the British government between the Foreign Office and the India Office. The preferred candidate of the latter was Ibn Saʿūd, the Wahhabi leader of the Nejd, a province lying along the eastern littoral of the Arabian Peninsula and thus an area that came under India Office jurisdiction.

The British Promise, 24 October 1915

A combination of military reverses and official predilections thus set the stage for a radical change in British policy toward the Arabs. McMahon sent off urgent telegrams to London recommending a quick, positive response to Husayn in view of Faruqi's warnings. Relying on the expertise of the men on the spot, Foreign Secretary Sir Edward Grey granted McMahon unusually wide powers to "promise whatever necessary" to the Arabs. His single caveat was that nothing must be given away that might prejudice French interests in the area. With this carte blanche from London, McMahon proceeded, with the help of his oriental secretary, Storrs, to write Husayn the key letter in the whole correspondence, dated 24 October 1915.

McMahon's letter is characterized by its ambiguity. It did not specify boundaries within which the British would recognize Arab independence; rather, it excluded from the areas demanded in Husayn's letter of the previous July those regions where Britain would not feel able to recognize Arab independence. The excluded areas fell into three categories: first, those the British did not regard as purely Arab by population; second, those in which Britain did not feel free to act because of French interests; and last, territories already in some form of treaty relationship with Britain.

Although the second category was potentially most prej-
udicial to Arab interests, and indeed at the time caused the
greatest discussion and disharmony, it was the first category that later gave grounds for the most polemics. It is
worth quoting from that part of McMahon's letter excluding territories assessed by the British as not purely Arab:

> The districts of Mersin and Alexandretta, and por-
> tions of Syria lying to the West of the districts of Da-
> mascus, Homs, Hama and Aleppo, cannot be said to
> be purely Arab, and must on that account be excepted
> from the proposed delimitation.[7]

Around this single sentence there has since raged an
Arab-Zionist polemic as to whether the area later known
as Mandated Palestine was in fact excluded from the areas
assigned to Husayn in October 1915. Here I propose first
to analyze the text itself and to try by deduction to determine the only possible interpretation that would make
sense; next I shall try to determine the *motives* and *intentions* of those responsible for the letter of 24 October.

Confining ourselves to the text, we must first define the
meaning of the word *districts* as it refers to Damascus,
Homs, Hama, and Aleppo. The area of the four towns had
been mentioned first by Faruqi. One historian has even referred to them as delineating a natural border from north
to south, being the eastern limit of the crusaders' conquests
in the Middle Ages. The most relevant fact, however, seems
to be that Storrs translated the English *district* into the ambiguous *vilayet* (the Turkish adaptation of the Arabic *wi-
lāyah*). In Arabic, the word *vilayet* has several possible
meanings, as indeed does the English *district*. Like the En-

---

7. I have used the translation by Antonius, ibid., p. 419.

glish word, *vilayet* is capable of meaning either a precise administrative unit or, in a general sense, surroundings, suburbs, and, in Arabic, even a street. Not only the British side but also Husayn himself used the word *vilayet* in a confusing fashion. In Husayn's response to the letter of 24 October, he agreed to concede his claim to the *vilayet*s of Mersin and Adana. Here Husayn was probably using *vilayet* in the general sense of the word, as there was no *vilayet* (administrative district) of Mersin but only a *vilayet* of Adana, which contained the port and district of Adana.

How did the use of the word *vilayet* apply to the key sentence in the October letter? Isaiah Friedman has claimed that *vilayet* was used in the sense of administrative district and that "district of Damascus" referred in fact to the *vilayet* of Syria, given that *vilayet*s were sometimes named after their capital city. The *vilayet* of Syria stretched from a point north of Hama south to ʿAqaba; clearly Palestine lies to the west of that area and thus would have been excluded from the area promised to the Arabs.

But can this interpretation be upheld? Even a cursory examination of the text would indicate that it cannot. Four towns are mentioned: Damascus, Homs, Hama, and Aleppo. If we assume *vilayet* to mean an administrative unit, then not only Damascus but also the three other towns would have to be administrative units. A quick reference to map 1 shows immediately that there were no *vilayet*s of Homs and Hama—Homs was a subdistrict and Hama a district in the *vilayet* of Syria (Suriyya). Further, although there was indeed a *vilayet* of Aleppo, to the west of it lay either the sea or the already-mentioned territories of Mersin and Alexandretta.

Thus it is clear that, relying solely on the text as it stands, the words *district* and *vilayet* cannot possibly refer to an

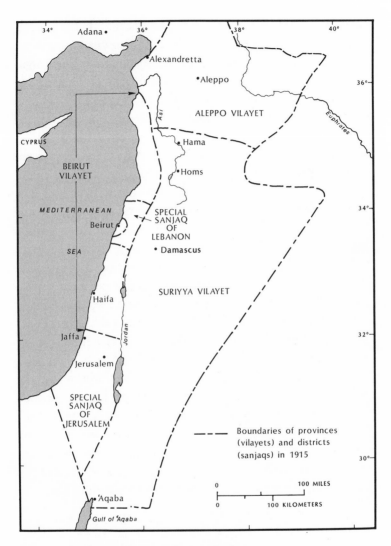

34°   Adana•   36°   38°   40°

•Alexandretta

•Aleppo   36°

ALEPPO VILAYET

CYPRUS   Asi   •Hama   Euphrates

BEIRUT
VILAYET   •Homs

MEDITERRANEAN   34°

SPECIAL
SANJAQ
OF
LEBANON

Beirut•

SEA   • Damascus

SURIYYA VILAYET

•Haifa   32°

Jaffa•   Jordan

•
Jerusalem

SPECIAL
SANJAQ
OF
JERUSALEM

Boundaries of provinces
(vilayets) and districts
(sanjaqs) in 1915   30°

0   100 MILES

•'Aqaba

Gulf of 'Aqaba   0   100 KILOMETERS

Map 1. Ottoman Syria, 1517–1918

administrative unit but must mean "district" in the general sense—that is, the environs of the four towns in question. An area to the west of a line drawn through the four towns would approximate today's Lebanon, leaving Palestine in the area assigned by McMahon to the Arabs.

Unfortunately, we cannot stop at a simple analysis of the text itself. First, there are serious grounds for doubting whether Storrs (aided by a Kurd named Ruhi) really grasped the potential meanings of the word *vilayet*. Storrs's memoirs raise grave doubts about his proficiency in Arabic.[8] The roots of what later became a monumental dispute may thus lie in a translation error committed by a British official whose Arabic was not quite as good as he thought it was.

Further, the archives have since revealed that the McMahon letter of 24 October 1915 was little more than a cynical emergency measure, taken to lure the Arabs out of the Turkish camp. The only contemporary criticism of McMahon came from his old colleagues at the India Office, who resented the far-reaching promises being made to a relatively obscure desert sheikh. The India Office was at the time waging war in Mesopotamia, which it hoped to annex to the Indian empire. McMahon's promise made special arrangements for Mesopotamia but did not exclude it from the area of ultimate Arab independence. When the viceroy of India complained to McMahon in November 1915, he received the following confidential explanation:

> I do not for one moment go to the length of imagining that the present negotiations will go far to shape the future form of Arabia or to either establish our rights

---

8. See the scathing remarks of Elie Kedourie on Storrs's Arabic, as reflected in his memoirs (*Orientations* [London, 1943]), in Elie Kedourie, *In the Anglo-Arab Labyrinth* (Cambridge, 1976), pp. 99–100.

or to bind our hands in that country. . . . What we have to arrive at now is to tempt the Arab people into the right path, detach them from the enemy and bring them to our side. . . . This on our part is at present largely a matter of words and to succeed we must use persuasive terms and abstain from haggling over conditions—whether about Baghdad or elsewhere.[9]

This confidential note is sufficient to indicate the worth of McMahon's later denials that he ever intended to include Palestine in the area allotted to the Arabs. On one occasion McMahon claimed disingenuously that he had chosen to demarcate the Arab territory along the line of the four towns because he had been unable to think of any other places at the time!

It must be remembered that later British denials that Palestine had been included in the areas promised to the Arabs (not always made with conviction) came after the issue of the Balfour Declaration, which, as we shall see, promised the Jews certain rights in Palestine. In 1915, when McMahon wrote his famous letter, the Zionist cause had yet to become an issue in international diplomacy, and the British saw no reason to solicit the aid of the Jews. But after 1917 the British could no more admit that they had promised Palestine first to the Arabs and then to the Jews than they could confess that McMahon's letter of 24 October 1915 had been a cynical sham.

The Arabs of Palestine, who had but recently become politically active, were exposed to the competing ideologies of renascent Islam, Ottomanism, Arabism, and Palestinian particularism. They did not become organized as

9. McMahon-Hardinge, 5 December 1915, quoted in Kedourie, *In the Anglo-Arab Labyrinth*, p. 120.

a Palestinian nationalist movement until after the British mandate had been imposed and King Faysal I's short-lived greater Syria had been dissolved by the French in 1920.

A Summary Evaluation of the Correspondence

Whereas the British undoubtedly incurred some moral commitments to the cause of Arab independence in 1915, the Husayn-McMahon correspondence can in no sense be regarded as an agreement legally binding on either side. It must also be emphasized that, however one chooses to interpret the word *vilayet*, Husayn himself did not agree to the exclusion of any areas west of the four towns. The correspondence continued, and ended in January 1916, without any consensus on this point. The exchange of letters was supposed to have been the prelude to negotiations between the two sides, but such negotiations never materialized. The Sykes-Picot Agreement signed by Britain, France, and Russia in May 1916 still referred to negotiations already conducted with the Arabs and expressed the hope that such negotiations would proceed via the same channels as hitherto—that is, via the British. If the negotiations did not materialize, it was quite probably because the Arab revolt did not live up to Allied expectations and because the Allies, in contrast to the situation in September 1915, felt little incentive to offer further concessions to the Arabs.

Over what did the two sides disagree in 1915? Certainly, Palestine itself was not even mentioned, nor in fact did it yet exist as a geopolitical unit. There is some reason to believe that Husayn himself understood the four-towns formula to refer to what is now Lebanon, for in his reply to McMahon's letter of 24 October he asserted that the Christian Arabs of that area were as much Arabs as the Muslims. In regard to this area Husayn agreed to suspend negotiations until after the war, in view of what he understood to be the special wartime bonds uniting Britain and France. But McMahon did not allow this assumption to go unchallenged. In January 1916, in his last letter of the series, McMahon warned Husayn not to harbor any illusions that the situation might change after the war, when Britain's ties with France would be even stronger, McMahon asserted, cemented further by the blood each country had shed in their joint war effort.

There was also Foreign Secretary Grey's caveat reserving areas that lay in the French sphere of interest. As far back as 1912 Grey himself had acknowledged in public that Ottoman Syria was an area of French interest. Again, during the negotiations between the Allies in March 1915 (known as the Constantinople Agreement), the French had laid claim to all of Ottoman Syria in the anticipated share-out of what had been Ottoman provinces in the Middle East. Although the French demand had not been conceded in toto in March 1915, it is clear that Grey's caveat in October of that year, and McMahon's reservations in his letter to Husayn, had the effect of mortgaging Arab independence in Syria to the ultimate arbitration of the French. However, as George Antonius has claimed, with much logic, even if McMahon did mean to reserve Palestine for the French, the fact that the French did not take possession of Palestine after the war should have annulled the "French reservation" on Palestine and allowed its natural reversion to the Arabs.

Of a more fundamental nature are the questions regarding the extent to which Husayn really represented Arab interests, or an "Arab nation," and the extent to which the Arabs themselves fulfilled *their* part of the agreement. I have already indicated that the Hashemites did not join the

Arab nationalist movement until inspired by British hints about the caliphate in 1915. The secret societies in Damascus clutched at the Hashemites as their last chance, hoping that the Hashemites' good contacts with the British would get them out of their own political and military impasse. The Hashemite-Syrian alliance was a marriage of convenience and, like most arrangements of this nature, was soon subject to second thoughts and misgivings. Toward the end of the war, with British armies rolling up the Turkish front in Syria, nationalist leaders in that country were concerned not to fall under Hashemite rule. The well-known appeal by seven Syrian leaders for self-rule, made to the British in Cairo in 1918, referred not to the Wilsonian principle of self-rule, as has so often been claimed, but rather to Syrian self-government as opposed to British-sponsored Hashemite rule.

Finally, the question of the Arab revolt's military value to the Allies may be touched upon briefly. In his letter of 24 October 1915 McMahon expressed the hope that his proposal would result in a "lasting and solid alliance" with the Arabs, of which one of the immediate consequences would be the expulsion of the Turks from the Arab countries. This hint of immediate action did not in fact suit the sharif, who in his next letter indicated that there were certain risks to be considered. In the first place, premature action might provoke an adverse reaction in the Arab and Muslim world to the Hashemites' revolt against the caliph; Husayn also feared to commit himself as yet to the Allied cause, not yet convinced that the Entente could overcome the Central Powers. Husayn knew he was dependent on outside forces to make good Arab claims, and precisely because of this he had to weigh the odds most carefully before committing himself to one side or the other.

Husayn did finally proclaim the Arab revolt, but only in June 1916, once convinced, wrongly, that a Turco-German expeditionary force into Arabia had in fact come to subdue the Hijaz and to depose him. The revolt made initial gains in the Hijaz but after a few short months had to be bailed out by the British. The main role performed by the Arab irregulars, trained by T. E. Lawrence and the less well known Captain H. Garland, was the sabotage of the Hijaz railway connecting Turkey with the Turkish army garrison in Medina. The efficacy of their operations may be gauged by the fact that the besieged garrison at Medina held out until after the war ended, provisioned all that time by the Hijaz railway link.

Once the final British campaign to conquer Syria got under way in 1917 under General Edmund Allenby's command, Arab irregulars under Faysal's command served as Allenby's right wing as he progressed northward. During this campaign the Arabs never once engaged the Turkish army in any set-piece battle, and, of course, could not have been expected to do so. The Turks were in retreat by 1918, and many towns were occupied without resistance. Arab observers have themselves recalled how British forces would halt at the outskirts of a town and allow the Arabs to enter first as triumphant conquerors. This was a political maneuver by the British to support Arab claims against the French by maintaining that the Arabs had indeed fulfilled their part of the agreement and earned the area of the four towns by conquest.

As for the contribution of the Palestinian Arabs, a recent study by the historian A. L. Tibawi claims that the first group of Palestinians was recruited to the revolt in July 1918. Some 125 men volunteered, but we are not informed whether they in fact managed to serve in the final campaign for the conquest of Damascus in October 1918, with which the war against the Turks in the Middle East came effectively to an end. If the Arab contribution in the military campaign waged by modern armies in the Middle East was modest, however, it is a fact that the invading British armies encountered little or no indigenous hostility during their campaigns. There is no way to determine which factors—fears of Ottoman repression and the benefits expected from the British, or the inspiration of the Arab revolt—were most responsible for the Arabs' benevolent neutrality.

I have tried to lay bare the anomalies and the ambiguities in Arab-British relations during World War I. It was basically on Britain's word, given in a single letter by a relatively minor official, that the Hashemites, and later the Palestinian Arabs, would base their political aspirations. They relied somewhat naively on the assurances of an imperial power that was unconscionably willing, when caught up in the exigencies of a global struggle, to scatter promises to minor actors in the greater drama with little or no thought for future consequences.

CHAPTER TWO

Zionism and the Balfour Declaration

Emancipation and Anti-Semitism

The emancipation (or political liberation) of the Jews was preceded by the Jewish Enlightenment (Haskalah, or spiritual liberation). During the eighteenth century the Jews of Western Europe, especially in Germany, began to emerge from their ghettos and to partake of the secular culture of their host nations. They discarded many religious practices, and the reform movement in Germany introduced a denominationalism similar to that which had split the Christian church.

The political emancipation of the Jews followed in the wake of the French Revolution. In 1791 the revolutionary national assembly removed all remaining legal restrictions on French Jews and recognized them as full citizens. Laws that distinguished between different religions seemed anomalous in the new age of liberalism. In 1807 Napoleon convened the ancient rabbinical assembly known as the Sanhedrin. The assembled rabbis took the historically inevitable step of proclaiming that the civil laws of the state and its military needs overrode all contrary prescriptions of the Jewish religion. Subsequent rabbinical conferences held in France affirmed that the Jews did not constitute a political nation but rather a unique spiritual community.

The 1860s were perhaps the most "liberal" decade of that century. Alexander II of Russia embarked on a series of reforms, the most significant of which was the emancipation of the serfs; in 1859 liberal majorities took control of the Prussian legislative assemblies; in 1867 Austria-Hungary liberalized itself into a multinational empire; and in the same year Disraeli granted the franchise to the urban proletariat in England.

The emancipation of the Jews had by now spread to most of Europe, as far east as Russia and to Rumania in the south. Culturally and socially the Jews of Europe attained the highest summits. Benjamin Disraeli (albeit baptized) was prime minister in England. In France, Adolphe (Isaac) Cremieux was the first practicing Jew to become a government minister; Achille Fould administered the finances of France, while the Rothschilds and the Péreire brothers built up its credit system. In Germany, Ferdinand Lassalle created the German labor movement. And from London, German-born Karl Marx presided over the First International.

Ironically, the first Zionist theorists, the precursors of Zionism, also appeared in this decade. Their call to the Jews to return to their ancient homeland in Palestine came precisely when the Jews of Europe were savoring to the full the fruits of emancipation. The reduced social need of the 1860s was indeed reflected in the writings of these early theorists—men such as the Orthodox rabbis Jehuda Alkalai (1798–1878); Zevi Hirsch Kalischer (1795–1874); and Moses Hess (1812–1875), a German Jew who exerted an intellectual influence on Marx and Engels and who was inspired by the Italian *risorgimento* to predict a Jewish national revival (*Rome and Jerusalem*, 1862). The physical and spiritual malaise of the Jews, a central motif in later Zionist writings, was not emphasized in their writings, and unlike the first *political* Zionists Pinsker and Herzl (see below), the precursors proposed a return to Zion not as a substitute for the emancipation but rather as a complement to it. Their call remained unanswered, however—the Jews were not yet ready to sacrifice the hope of assimilation into Western society for an unknown future in a backward province of the Ottoman empire.

But the 1860s proved to be a false dawn, and in many countries reaction set in soon enough. Over 80 percent of European Jewry resided within the Russian empire and in Eastern Europe. For them the progress of emancipation was altogether different from that granted their counterparts in the West. In Russia especially it had been slow and halting, and eventually it was aborted completely. It had been assumed that Tsar Alexander II would pursue his reforms to their logical conclusion, ultimately converting Russia into a constitutional monarchy on the Western model. In that process Jews might be granted free entry into society, as had been the case in the West. But all such illusions were shattered when Alexander was assassinated in 1881, and reaction set in. A wave of pogroms afflicted Russian Jewry, an experience as significant for them as the French Revolution had been for Western Jewry. The pogroms precipitated a flood of Jewish emigration to the West, primarily to the United States, with just a trickle to Palestine.

The most significant intellectual response to the pogroms was the publication of a small pamphlet called *Auto-*

Emancipation by a Russian Jewish physician named Leo Pinsker, who had himself observed the participation of Russian liberal intellectuals in the pogroms in Odessa. Pinsker concluded that anti-Semitism could not be dismissed simply as an anachronism left over from the Middle Ages that might be expected to disappear with the coming of the Enlightenment. He posited that the Jews were immutably alien in gentile society and concluded that the emancipation contrived for the Jews by gentile society could never work. The Jews would have to emancipate themselves, in their own land. As Herzl later quipped, the Jews might try to flee anti-Semitism, but they carried it along with them in their baggage.

Yet the appeal of Zionism to the Jewish masses was very limited. Of those who participated in the great migrations west, a mere 3 percent on average chose Palestine. The lack of congenial conditions (climate, political regime) in Palestine worked against the absorption of many who did make the journey. Failing to acclimatize to the harsh conditions, many reemigrated. Instead of assured individual emancipation in the West, Zionism offered only the ill-defined prospect of collective, national transformation in the future. Given the objective conditions in Palestine itself, the country could not possibly have solved the problems facing European Jews at the end of the nineteenth century. Zionism as a political movement would have no significant effect on the demography of the Jewish people for decades to come.

Political Zionism

It is somewhat ironic that until late in the nineteenth century the great powers evinced more interest in Palestine than the Jews themselves did. As European interest in the

Ottoman empire grew, the United States and all the major European powers opened consulates in Jerusalem. Articles in the British press advocated the reestablishment of the Jews in a state of their own in Palestine, perhaps as a buffer under British influence between Egypt and the Turks.

Gentile support for a return of the Jews to their ancient homeland was prompted not only by material and strategic interests but also by deep-rooted biblical tradition—a belief in the Protestant mission to compensate the Jews for Christian persecutions during their long exile. But gentile Zionists were never more than a small, if active, minority. Mainstream Christian thought adhered to the legend of the Wandering Jew, rejected by God because of his perfidy and doomed to exile in subjection to Christians for all time.

During the period from 1840 to 1880, when the Ottoman regime was sustained primarily by Britain, there were occasions when the Turks seemed to want Jewish settlers more than the Jews themselves wished to sponsor settlement. Ironically, it was during the last quarter of the century, when the Jews themselves first developed a serious impulse to settle in Palestine, that the Turks, in turning against Britain, turned also against Jewish colonization. After the Congress of Berlin in 1878, when the Western powers once more propped up the Ottomans against Russian encroachment, the Turks became even more resentful of the traditional privileges enjoyed by foreigners under the capitulations system (whereby foreigners were exempted from Turkish law).

By the close of the century Britain itself had come to regard the protection of the Jews as an obstacle to its continued good relations with the Sublime Porte. When approached by Herzl at the turn of the twentieth century, the British proposed alternatives to Palestine in British-controlled territories—at first in El Arish in the Sinai desert and then in East Africa.[1]

Political Zionism began in Russia as a clandestine movement in reaction to the 1881 pogroms. The Lovers of Zion (Hovevei Tsion) was formed in 1884 under Pinsker's leadership. Its goal was to promote and finance emigration to Palestine, and its members acted under the guise of a philanthropic organization to avoid censure or arrest by the Russian authorities. It took a Western Jew, Theodor Herzl, to place Zionism on the international political stage and to secure European recognition for Zionism as the movement for the national liberation of the Jews.

Herzl was a rare, if not unique, combination of playwright and statesman, with the audacity to practice diplomacy in the name of a people as yet without its own country. He freed Zionism from the constraints of timid, piecemeal colonization in Palestine and transformed it into a force to be reckoned with in world politics. This transformation would bring vital dividends when the Jews' opportunity came in World War I.

Herzl himself testified (in 1899) that he had been converted to Zionism by the trial and degradation of Captain Alfred Dreyfus, a Jewish officer in the French army who in 1895 was tried on trumped-up charges of treason, found guilty, and sentenced to imprisonment on Devil's Island. Recent research indicates, however, that Herzl put together this version after the event, that in fact he, together with most of French Jewry at the time, believed in Dreyfus's guilt

1. See Barbara Tuchman, *The Bible and the Sword: England and Palestine from the Bronze Age to Balfour* (London, 1956): and Walter Z. Laqueur, *A History of Zionism* (London, 1972).

at the time of the first trial. Indeed, the anti-Semitic implications of the Dreyfus trial did not come to light until
1896—*after* Herzl had written his Zionist tract *The Jewish State*. Herzl's conversion was prompted, rather, by the
progress of anti-Semitism in his own hometown, Vienna; a
visit there in September 1895 seems to have inspired *The
Jewish State*. Vienna was thus the cradle both of modern
anti-Semitism and of modern Zionism.[2]

The ideas put forward in Herzl's booklet were not original, but they were expressed with unusual clarity, daring,
and energy. The book reflected Herzl's gifts as one of Europe's leading journalists. It can be divided into two parts:
first, an analysis of anti-Semitism, or rather the Jewish position as affected by it; and second, a blueprint for organized settlements in the future Jewish territory and the mo-
bilization of both international political support and the
necessary finances. Herzl rejected the furtive methods of
the Lovers of Zion. Instead of a few individuals stealing in,
he wanted internationally recognized or guaranteed mass
migration.

Herzl dissipated his energies and finances trying to extract an official charter from the Ottoman sultan. The latter was willing to consider Jewish immigration, but he insisted that the Jews adopt Ottoman citizenship and scatter
their colonies across the empire—Palestine last of all. Although the sultan was indeed tempted by Jewish loans for
his bankrupt empire, he did not relish the idea of import-
ing another minority problem; nor did he wish to stir up
Arab nationalism. Negotiations with Herzl were broken off

2. See Jacques Kornberg, "Theodor Herzl: A Reevaluation," *Jour-
nal of Modern History* 52 (June 1980): 226–252; and Henry Cohn,
"Theodor Herzl's Conversion to Zionism," *Jewish Social Studies* 32
(January 1970): 101–110.

in 1902 when the sultan accepted a French loan. Herzl realized that he had been played off against the French all along. But he had himself been bluffing in his offers of Jewish loans to the Ottomans—none of the Jewish notables Herzl approached had been willing to advance him the cash with which to finance the loans. Nevertheless, for years afterward Herzl claimed that he could have gotten Palestine if only the rich Jews had put up the money.·

Herzl's disillusion with Jewish notables caused him to turn to the Jewish masses. In 1897, publication of a new Zionist newspaper, *Die Welt,* edited of course by Herzl, commenced. Then in August 1897 Herzl convened the First Zionist Congress (initially called "The Society of the Jews") in Basel, Switzerland. Over half the nearly two hundred delegates came from Eastern Europe, nearly a quarter from Russia. Their principal common attribute was membership in the Lovers of Zion. Covered as it was by the world press, the congress made a great impression on the international scene.

Zionist congresses became routine affairs, held annually until 1901, and then biannually. By 1900 there were over a thousand local affiliated Zionist organizations, over a hundred in the United States alone. But again rich Jews did not support the movement. Funds collected by subscription proved insufficient to establish the colonial trust decided upon at the first congress. Although the masses took to the majesty of Herzl, the Russian Zionists, by far the largest faction, came to resent his autocratic methods and the way he placed the movement's executive bodies under the control of his cronies. The Russians organized a "Democratic Faction" opposition, led by, among others, a young chemist who would himself one day lead the world movement and become first president of the state of Israel—

Chaim Weizmann. Socialist Zionists (and there were many) criticized the new movement; in their opinion it was dominated by "the bourgeoisie, religious elements, and rotten intellectuals."

But with all its internal bickering and weakness, the new movement gave Herzl a large popular backing and an institutional base for his diplomatic activity. Following the collapse of his negotiations in Turkey, he approached the British. In October 1902 he was received by the colonial secretary, Joseph Chamberlain, who agreed to consider the establishment of a self-governing Jewish colony at the southeastern corner of the Mediterranean. The El Arish strip at the edge of the Sinai was considered but rejected by the authorities in Egypt, because the colony would have had to draw off large quantities of Nile water for irrigation. Herzl was spurred to greater effort when further pogroms in Kishinev in 1903 underscored the urgency of the Jewish plight. In April 1903 Chamberlain, just returned from East Africa, proposed the dispatch of a commission of inquiry to examine the suitability of that territory for Jewish colonization.

Herzl laid Chamberlain's proposal before the Sixth Zionist Congress, the last he would attend. He claimed that the "Uganda Scheme" (in fact, the territory lay in what subsequently became Kenya) was only an emergency measure to provide immediate relief for Jewish suffering. His colleague Max Nordau called it a *Nachtasyl* (night shelter). The plenary session cheered Herzl, but widespread opposition was expressed when the various factions met in separate caucuses. The Russians in particular refused to be diverted from Palestine, even temporarily, and resented being told that Zion was a dream, that redemption must come from Uganda.

Serious objections to Herzl's diplomatic efforts were raised by Asher Ginzberg (1856–1927), a leader of "Spiritual Zionism" known as Ahad Ha'am ("One of the People") whose ideas had a profound influence upon Weizmann, although they were never accepted by the Jewish masses. Subjectively Ahad Ha'am rejected the Diaspora as an unpleasant evil; but objectively he accepted the evident fact that Jews could, and would, continue to live in the Diaspora for the foreseeable future. In his view the Jews' salvation would come from the prophets, not the diplomats— from an early stage the Jewish prophets had taught respect for the power of the spirit and had opposed the worship of material power.

Ahad Ha'am concluded that only a spiritual center in Palestine would be able to care for the needs of those Jews who were perforce left in the Diaspora. On this ground he criticized Herzl's 1896 tract for not specifying the geographical location of the Jewish state. And later on he derided Herzl's vision of a Jewish utopia (*Altneuland*, 1902) where the Jews spoke German or French: this might be established as the Jews' state, but it would not become a Jewish state in the sense of a center of identification for those Jews who remained outside it. There was also a pragmatic side to the aloof intellectual. Ahad Ha'am was one of the first to comment on the Arab problem and to foresee that the Jews could never succeed in building some tranquil Jewish Switzerland (as Herzl envisaged) in the center of the Arab Middle East.

At the Sixth Zionist Congress Herzl was called a traitor to his face. Although his personal prestige ensured a majority in favor of the British commission to Uganda, it was clear that the Russian Zionists would not go there. A conference of Russian Zionists at Kharkov passed a resolution accusing Herzl of having violated the Basel program. The Zionist movement outside Russia believed the Russians were trying to depose Herzl. In response Herzl taunted the Lovers of Zion—they might buy up all of Palestine piecemeal, but it would still remain Turkish territory.

Herzl was reconciled with the Russians in 1904. He promised not to exert any further pressure over Uganda, and they agreed to decide on the issue according to the facts. But Herzl was a broken man, both spiritually and physically. He died in 1904, before the next congress accorded the Uganda scheme an official burial. Herzl's heart condition had not been known to the Jewish masses, nor did they learn of the internal bickering. During his short Zionist career Herzl had come to be regarded as the uncrowned king of the Jews, and he was accorded a hero's funeral, mourned by hundreds of thousands.

How should we summarize Herzl's achievements? By his own standards he was a failure, never achieving the diplomatic breakthrough he yearned for. Herzl himself has left a hint that his whole Zionist endeavor was but a distraction from his true calling, a literary career, which eluded him. Just two years before his death, Herzl made the following confession to his diary:

> Sometimes it happens that a man of worth is active in several fields. Then he is certain to be recognized only in the field that is peripheral to the real centre of his personality. Thus, for example, I have become world famous in a sphere where I have accomplished next to nothing intellectually, but have merely displayed a mediocre political skill attainable by anyone with a grain of horse sense, in a matter which only blockheads cannot find crystal clear—there, in the Jewish Question. I have become a renowned propagandist. But as an au-

thor, particularly as a playwright, I am held to be nothing. I am merely called a journalist.

And I feel, I know, that I am by instinct a great writer, or was one, who failed to yield his full harvest only because he became fed up and discouraged.[3]

At his death, Herzl had indeed become an anachronism whose desperate drive to achieve a diplomatic breakthrough had cut him off from the masses he had originally inspired. After his death the Zionist movement retreated into the political doldrums, and, like the Arabs, had to await the cataclysm of World War I to achieve its next breakthrough.

But Herzl's efforts had laid the foundations, ensuring that the Jews would be able to take their chance when it came. He had transformed Zionist endeavor from the narrow cultural renaissance of a few individuals who incidentally engaged in philanthropic colonization into a political movement, centrally organized in several countries. Herzl had brought together the forces of Jewry in Eastern and Western Europe.

After Herzl's death the Zionist movement focused on consolidating its colonization efforts in Palestine itself. The socialist Zionist settlers of the second *aliya* (immigration wave—literally, "going up") established the foundations of a Jewish working and peasant class in Palestine. It included in its ranks most of the first generation of Israel's statesmen and leaders. Yet by the eve of World War I, the Zionists' achievements in Palestine were notable for their quality rather than quantity. Between 1882 and 1914 some 100,000 Jews had come to Palestine—but over half had left again. Of the 80,000 Jews in Palestine in 1914, some 30,000 were either

3. Diary entry for 4 June 1902, *The Complete Diaries of Theodor Herzl,* ed. Raphael Patai (New York, 1960), 4:1283.

expelled by the Turks or fled during the war (most of the latter returned at the war's end). Over the same period, however, the Arab community enjoyed a remarkable natural increase—from 300,000 in 1881 to about 600,000 by 1918. Of these, some 10 percent were Christians, and the vast majority were Sunni Muslims. The 1922 British census of Palestine recorded a population of 660,000 Arabs (589,000 Muslims and 71,000 Christians) and 83,000 Jews.[4]

The Balfour Declaration

In his memoirs, written some twenty years after the event, ex–Prime Minister David Lloyd George invented the myth that the Balfour Declaration had been a reward given to Weizmann in return for the latter's wartime services (in the field of explosives) to England. When Weizmann came to write his own memoirs, he commented wryly that he wished it had been as simple as that. Nonetheless, the myth has persisted.

This apocryphal version not only is flattering to Weizmann, but it also wrongly places the initiative with the Jews rather than with the British government. The Balfour Declaration was calculated to further very concrete *British* interests; certainly it was not simply a personal "gift" awarded to a gifted Jewish scientist by an appreciative prime minister. The negotiations that culminated in the declaration began in February 1917. They were initiated by the British, not by the Zionists, and it was not sheer coincidence that the head of the British team was Sir Mark Sykes, negotiator of the May 1916 Anglo-French (Sykes-Picot) agreement to partition the Middle East. Why did the British turn

4. *Royal Commission (Peel) Report,* Cmd. 5479, July 1937, pp. 13, 43.

now to the Zionists, some fourteen years after the abortive Herzl-Chamberlain negotiations on East Africa?

In 1917 the British had very solid strategic reasons for seeking an understanding with the Zionists. The Lloyd George government, which came to power in December 1916, was looking for a military victory in the East and planned the conquest of Ottoman Syria from its base in Egypt. Palestine itself had assumed an enhanced strategic importance during the war. Hitherto, British planning had relied on the desert wastes of Sinai to interpose an impenetrable land barrier between the all-important Suez Canal and any enemy approaching from the north. But that particular myth had been shattered in February 1915 when a Turkish force guided by German experts had successfully crossed the Sinai and reached the canal. The Turkish army in fact achieved nothing, apart from disrupting canal traffic for a day or two, but the psychological impact on British thinking was immense. By the end of 1915 the British garrison along the canal had been increased to 300,000.

Lloyd George felt that the previous government had ceded too much to the French under the Sykes-Picot Agreement. The negotiations that led to this agreement were in direct consequence of the correspondence then proceeding between McMahon and Husayn (see chapter 1). Indeed, in a sense it had been an attempt to square the British commitment to the Arabs with that to the French. Foreign Secretary Grey stated that an agreement with the French was a "wartime necessity." Following the British military defeat at the Dardanelles, Britain needed a new offensive in the Middle East and had first to reassure the French about its intentions. It was decided to tell the French about the negotiations with the Arabs and to predicate the promise of

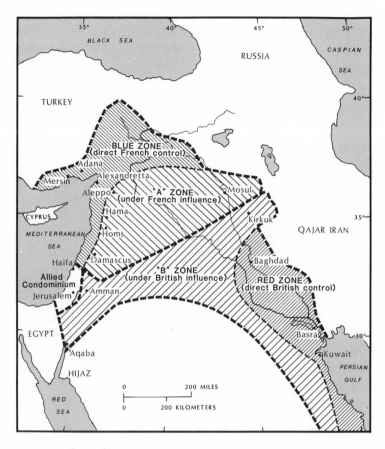

Map 2. The Sykes-Picot Agreement, May 1916

independence on the Arabs themselves giving serious proof of revolt.

The French agreed to cede to the Arabs a state in the Syrian interior east of the four towns Damascus, Homs, Hama, and Aleppo, though it has to be doubted whether they took the Arabs' claims seriously. The Arabs were thus to receive a state in which paramount influence would be exercised in the north (the Syrian interior) by the French and in the south (today's Jordan) by the British. In addition, the French were to exercise direct control over Lebanon, and the British over Iraq. The Sykes-Picot partition plan makes explicit mention of the independent Arab state to be established east of the four towns, each of which is mentioned by name.

Some critical discrepancies remain, however, between the British promise to the Arabs and their partition agreement with the French. Above all, in the context of our present discussion, the intended fate of Palestine is by no means clear. Under the Sykes-Picot plan, Palestine was to be administered by an international "condominium" of the English, French, and Russians (also signatories to the agreement), with the Haifa Bay area set aside as a British naval base. But it remains unclear whether Palestine was to be included in the independent Arab state. In any case, McMahon had, on the foreign secretary's instructions, stipulated that his offer was subject to there being no infringement of French interests.

The Sykes-Picot Agreement attained some notoriety after its publication. Yet its latter-day reputation hardly reflects the realities of the time. The Arabs had not enjoyed sovereignty for nearly four hundred years and must have expected (and before the war had elicited) some form of foreign tutelage, initially at least. But perhaps more to the point, British arms were about to release the Arabs from the Turkish yoke, and at that time it was generally accepted that victorious armies were entitled to political reward. Given the Middle Eastern "investment" of the Western powers, the mandate imposed later was perhaps inevitable. Indeed, it would seem that the Arab state established in Syria objected not so much to the system as to the proprietor it was given—the French. Events would take an entirely different course in Palestine, of course, but in 1916 no one was yet giving much thought to the Zionists' future role in the area.

The Lloyd George cabinet decided that the eastern approaches to the Suez Canal could be safeguarded adequately only if the land barrier extended northward into Palestine. (Lloyd George would also demand from the French the return of the Mosul area of northern Iraq, acquired by France under the Sykes-Picot Agreement.) The idea of using the Jews to safeguard British imperial interests in the Middle East had been proposed in the cabinet by Lord Herbert Samuel (who was president of the Local Government Board) in March 1915, but it had been rejected by the Asquith government. In 1916 Lloyd George favored sponsorship of the Jews, the more so if they, the Jews, could help the British extricate themselves from the Sykes-Picot Agreement.

British support for Zionism could be presented to the world as an enlightened, idealistic policy pressed on them by the Jews. The French would be unable to accuse them of reneging on a solemn agreement out of narrrow self-interest. Furthermore, President Wilson, who had to be satisfied that the Allies' war aims were "honorable" before he committed the United States, might be persuaded that the British were not about to colonize Palestine out of narrow imperial interest but that in returning the "people of

the Bible" to the "land of the Bible" they were in fact pro-
moting the cause of Jewish autonomy. Sponsorship of Zionism might thus at one and the same time get the British out
of a tight corner with the French and fit in with the American president's conception of a new world order.

Following the first meetings between Sykes and the Zionists in February 1917, the Russian Zionist leader Nahum
Sokolow was designated a "roving ambassador" to sell the
idea to Britain's allies. Sokolow visited Paris and told the
French government that the Zionists preferred a British
single-power protectorate in Palestine. The French, suspect-
ing a British ruse to extricate themselves from the Sykes-
Picot Agreement, initially balked at the idea. But the French,
like the Italians (and the British for that matter), believed
in the need to harness Jewish influence to the Allied cause,
and they eventually endorsed the project.

Herzl had already put Zionism on the world map and
done much to convince the powers that Zionism was supported by world Jewry. Thus, in 1917 all the powers believed that support for the return of the Jews to Palestine
would in turn harness the alleged international influence
and power of the Jews on behalf of the sponsor. Even if the
Jews' power was no more than a myth, the important point
is that statesmen such as Lloyd George believed in it. Naturally, the Zionists themselves did nothing to disabuse Western statesmen, for the myth in this instance enhanced their
own bargaining power with the Allies. Significantly, both
France and England included Jewish "advisers" in their
wartime missions to the United States.

The need for every extra bit of leverage was crucial for
England in 1917, the worst year of the war for the Allies.
Not only was Germany beginning to starve England by
submarine warfare in the Atlantic, but also the Russian

war effort on the Eastern Front had deteriorated rapidly as that country was racked internally by revolution. Most important, the Americans had yet to send a single soldier to help out in Europe.

Lloyd George himself testified later that the need to mobilize American resources and to keep the Russians in the war was all but overpowering in 1917. It was believed that public opinion in both countries would play a decisive role and that the friendliness or hostility of the Jews might turn the scales in either direction. The Jews were thought to dominate the Russian revolutionary movement and to be among President Wilson's most influential advisers.

As we now know, the United States did in fact declare war on Germany (though not on the Turks) in April 1917, long before the negotiations with the Jews had reached the stage of drafting a document. Yet even then the Zionists were able to demonstrate their "influence." In May 1917 the Americans tried to secure a separate peace with the Turks. The British and Zionists shared a common interest in opposing this move, which, if successful, would have left Palestine in Turkish hands. Weizmann was rushed by the British to Gibraltar, where he was able to dissuade the American envoy, Henry Morgenthau, a Jew, from pursuing his mission further. Moreover, when it came to securing American endorsement of the Balfour Declaration, another Jew, Chief Justice Louis Brandeis, was instrumental in obtaining Wilson's assent.

The benefits gained by Britain from the Zionist movement in Russia were less tangible. The Russian Zionist movement did not support the proposed British declaration, although there was general rejoicing among Russian Jews when it was issued in November 1917. The fifteen or twenty Jews among the higher echelons of the Bolshevik party proved to be anti-Zionist, and after the October Revolution the new government soon denounced Zionism as a capitalist contrivance.

The myth of Jewish influence played a key role in one more quarter. The British became convinced (thanks to an assiduous Jewish lobby that supplied the government with press clippings) that if they did not issue a pro-Zionist declaration, the Germans would preempt them. On 24 October 1917, Sir Ronald Graham, head of the Eastern Department at the Foreign Office, warned that the Zionists might be thrown into the arms of the Germans unless an assurance of sympathy was given to them (a corollary of Faruqi's warnings in Cairo in September 1915; see above, p. 17). British fears of a German declaration dominated the conclusive cabinet meeting at the end of October when the final draft of the declaration was approved.

Wartime military desiderata thus combined with projected imperial designs in 1917. But there was also a strong domestic motive, frequently overlooked by historians. The predicament of Russian Jewry had been of some concern to British statesmen over the previous two to three decades. First, the flight of Jews from Russian pogroms to the liberal West had provoked acute social problems in England itself. Anti-Semitic reaction to the East European ghetto communities in 1904–1905 had prompted the Balfour administration to legislate restrictions on aliens.

Next, Russian Jews were held responsible toward the latter stages of the war for the revolutionary and anarchic tendencies that engulfed Russia. Many gentile Zionists in the British establishment were motivated in part by the hope that a Jewish national home would convert the Jews into a "normal" people, thus relieving England, and the world, of the disorders caused by an unstable community.

Members of the established Jewish community in England, many of whom had won for themselves eminent positions in British social and political life, were concerned as much as anyone by the manifestations of anti-Semitism, fearing that it would disturb their own privileged positions. Some of these themes are touched on in a contemporary letter written by Leo Amery, a secretary to the imperial war cabinet who, with Lord Alfred Milner (a member of the cabinet without portfolio), was largely responsible for drafting the final British text of the Balfour Declaration:

> Once there is a national home for the Jewish persecuted majority, the English Jews will no longer have anything to trouble about. On the other hand, an anti-Semitism which is based partly on the fear of being swamped by hordes of undesirable aliens from Russia, etc., and partly by an instinctive suspicion against a community which has so many international ramifications, will be much diminished when the hordes in question have got another outlet, and when the motive for internationalism among the Jews is diminished.[5]

And, finally, one cannot discount the religious impact of a project to reinstate the Jews in their ancient homeland. Both Lloyd George and Balfour were devout churchgoers who knew their Bible well; the former told Weizmann that he knew the map of the Holy Land better than he did that

5. Leo Amery to Sir Edward Carson, a member of the imperial war cabinet, 4 September 1917, in *The Leo Amery Diaries,* vol. 1: *1896– 1929,* ed. John Barnes and David Nicholson (London, 1980), pp. 170–171. On the role played by Amery and Milner in the drafting of the declaration, see Amery's diary note of 31 October 1917, in ibid., pp. 169–170; and Leonard Stein, *The Balfour Declaration* (London, 1961), pp. 520–521. See also Michael J. Cohen, *Churchill and the Jews* (London, 1985), pp. 52–53, for elaboration on Amery's point.

of France. Balfour had been deeply impressed by Weizmann when the two first met in 1906 in Manchester. When Balfour had asked why the Jews were so attached to Palestine, Weizmann had asked, "Mr. Balfour, supposing I were to offer you Paris instead of London, would you take it?" Balfour had replied, "But Dr. Weizmann, we already have London." Weizmann responded, "That is true, but we had Jerusalem when London was a marsh."[6]

Yet it is probably fair to say that Balfour's and Lloyd George's religious zeal took second place to their concern for the British empire. Their support for Zionism was given practical expression only after strategic interest pointed in that direction. Balfour would later advocate that the Americans take on the Palestine mandate. Neither man seems to have played an active role in writing the final draft of the declaration, whose terms were far from those suggested by the Zionists themselves and whose very ambiguity and vagueness bore the seeds of future conflict.

The Drafting and Significance of the Declaration

The Jewish establishment in England was wholly out of sympathy with Zionist aspirations and advised the Foreign Office to ignore them. Well-established families feared that the creation of a Jewish national entity in Palestine would force all English Jews to make the choice between their English citizenship and emigration to an unknown land. The majority of the Jewish elite regarded their Judaism as "a collection of abstract religious principles" and Zionism as "the empty dream of a few misguided idealists." However, the Jewish notables in England had lost touch with the Jewish masses, now swelled by tens of thousands of Russian

6. Chaim Weizmann, *Trial and Error* (New York, 1966), p. 111.

immigrants, for whom Weizmann and Zionism seemed to indicate the coming of the millennium.

In May 1917 the split between the Zionists and the Jewish establishment came out into the open. Following a public speech in which Weizmann referred to the anti-Zionists as a "small minority," two leaders of the Board of Deputies of British Jews published a letter in *The Times* reiterating their opposition to any theory of the Jews as a homeless nationality—which, if generally accepted, would effectively have stamped the Jews as strangers in their native lands. They warned that it would be a calamity if Jewish settlers in Palestine were to receive special rights such as political privileges or economic preferences—this would be in conflict with the principle of equal rights for all and would compromise the Jews wherever they had secured equal rights. It would also involve the Jews in Palestine in the most bitter of feuds with their Arab neighbors.

The letter to *The Times* proved counterproductive, and prominent Jewish leaders published a riposte dissociating themselves from it. The Board of Deputies passed a vote of no confidence in the Conjoint committee that had represented the Jews to the Foreign Office, forcing that body to dissolve itself. Thus the Jewish community in England rallied round the Zionists, who were able to present a united front to the British government.

However, the opposition of anti-Zionist Jews would have a crucial influence on the drafting of the Balfour Declaration. Opposition to the Zionist demands was voiced inside the cabinet itself by Edwin Montagu, a cousin of Lord Samuel's appointed in July 1917 to the position of secretary of state for India. On 18 July the Zionists, after much internal debate, submitted a draft formula to the government that considerably modified their original demand for the reconstitution of Palestine as a Jewish state. Instead, the Zionist draft asked the British government to recognize Palestine as "the National Home of the Jewish People."

Montagu fought a lone, but critically effective, rear-guard battle when the Zionist formula was discussed in the cabinet on 3 September 1917. In a memorandum entitled "The Anti-Semitism of the Present Government," he attacked the plan to issue a pro-Zionist statement. The issue was deferred while the draft was submitted for President Wilson's approval. Wilson's noncommittal reply only aggravated the issue further, however. The first full-dress debate on the declaration took place on 4 October. Montagu made a long, emotional appeal to his colleagues. He had, on 3 September, made the wild claim that Whitehall had become the instrument of an organization that was run largely by "men of enemy descent and birth." Now, on 4 October, he again cast almost racist aspersions on the Russian Jewish immigrants who formed the mainstay of the Zionist movement in England, claiming that *he* and *his kind* represented the true views of the indigenous Jewish community in England. He asked rhetorically how he was supposed to represent the views of the British government during his forthcoming visit to India if the same government declared that his national home was in Turkish territory. Montagu was supported by Lord Curzon, who questioned whether Palestine would be able to absorb large-scale Jewish immigration and asked how the Arab problem was to be solved.

Montagu's opposition did not change the cabinet's determination, but it did convince the Zionist sympathizers in the cabinet of the need for a compromise text in order to get the issue resolved without endless delays. The final draft was worked out by Lord Milner, one of Lloyd George's closest associates in the imperial war cabinet, and by Leo

Amery, who would be involved intimately with Palestine over the next three decades. Their textual amendments were designed to avert Arab opposition, which might be aroused if it seemed that a Christian power was "forcing" the realization of Jewish aims on Palestine, and they tried to accommodate the objections of the still-powerful non-Zionist Jews in England.

The final draft made certain critical amendments to the Zionists' draft of the previous July. First, in lieu of "recognizing Palestine as the national home of the Jewish People," His Majesty's Government would now "favour the establishment in Palestine of a national home for the Jewish People." The insertion of the indefinite article in place of the definite meant that instead of *all* Palestine being converted into a refuge for the Jews, the latter would have to be content with establishing their home in just a part of Palestine. How large that part would ultimately be no one could say in 1917; future political and military factors would determine this. In addition, the second paragraph of the Zionist draft, stipulating that the British government "regards as essential for the realization of this principle the grant of internal autonomy to the Jewish nationality in Palestine," was deleted. In its place the British inserted a new clause that made British aid to the Zionist cause conditional on "nothing being done which may prejudice the civil and religious rights of existing non-Jewish communities in Palestine, or the rights and political status enjoyed by Jews in any other country."

The provision for safeguarding the rights of the non-Jewish communities, clearly a sop to Montagu and the non-Zionist Jews in Britain, would have drastic long-term consequences. It has been argued that the Balfour Declaration arrogantly ignored the Arab presence in Palestine,

using the term "non-Jewish" rather than Arab and referring only to the Arabs' civil and religious, not political,
rights. The Jews would argue that the British obligation to
them preceded, and therefore must take precedence over,
any reference to the Arabs. Ironically, had it not been for
the opposition of the British Jews in 1917, there might never
have been any proviso regarding Arab rights in what was
originally intended to be a gesture of support for the Jews
in Palestine. Ultimately, Arab and Jewish interpretations of
the declaration would be of less importance than would the
use the British chose to make of it. The British never accepted the Zionist theory that the declaration was concerned primarily with Jewish rights in Palestine. In British
eyes the declaration would be regarded as a "dual obligation"—to both Jews and Arabs.

The Balfour Declaration Assessed, and Compared with the Husayn-McMahon Correspondence

The Balfour Declaration was received with great elation by
Jewish communities around the world, and with matching
trepidation by the Arab community in Palestine (where it
was published, belatedly, in March 1920). Undoubtedly, it
marked a turning point in the history of the Jewish people
and of Palestine itself.

But the hopes and fears it engendered were equally exaggerated. It fell fatally short of the Zionists' original hopes.
As a people without a territory who sought to return to
their ancient homeland, now occupied by an Arab majority and still in 1917 under Turkish suzerainty, the Jews had
since 1897 avoided the demand for a Jewish state. In 1917
the use of the euphemism "Jewish national home" compromised the Zionist cause. The very term was unknown in
international usage and was therefore open to different in-

terpretations according to one's persuasion. Once Montagu's protests led to the guarantee of Jewish rights *outside* Palestine, a parallel guarantee of non-Jewish rights *inside* Palestine was an obvious quid pro quo. Montagu's anxieties (he was reported to have been close to tears in the cabinet) reflected a fundamental sense of insecurity, for all the eminence of his position. The "guarantee" carried no legal authority and was quite meaningless. In the process the quid pro quo for the "non-Jewish communities" completely altered the nature of the declaration.

The Balfour Declaration was not only ambiguous but also fatally vague. No borders were established for the Jews' national home; no machinery was created whereby the British might "facilitate" its well-being and progress. Indeed, no one would ever be able to determine the extent of the British commitment or at what point it would be fulfilled.

The basic significance of the declaration was that it opened up new possibilities for the Zionist movement. It radically transformed the Zionists' international status and their position in Palestine itself, where the Jews, previously aliens, were now an officially recognized community granted certain privileges. The declaration gave the Jews their great chance—but the consummation of the Zionist enterprise would depend on their own ability to establish a viable Jewish community in Palestine and, in the process, to accommodate, or ultimately overcome, Arab opposition.

Both the Balfour Declaration and the Husayn-McMahon correspondence had their origins in British war interests. In each case Britain sought to promote its own war effort by mobilizing the aid of minor, if significant, allies. But whereas the Balfour Declaration focused on Palestine (albeit an undetermined part of it), the McMahon letter of

24 October 1915 made reference to all the Arab-inhabited lands of the Middle East and left room for later doubt as to whether it had been the intention to include Palestine or not. The British side at least, unable to admit any duplicity toward Jews and Arabs, maintained consistently, but often disingenuously, that Palestine had *not* been included in the area promised to the Arabs in 1915.

Another significant difference was that the Husayn-McMahon correspondence remained secret, whereas the Balfour Declaration was published on the day of its issue. The reason for the secrecy about the correspondence was not that the British feared revealing its implications for Palestine, as has often been claimed by the Arabs, but because the British feared an adverse reaction by the Muslim population of India, which might object to Britain plotting the overthrow of the caliph. The British finally published the text of the correspondence in 1939 at the behest of the Arabs attending the St. James conference on Palestine.

In contrast, the Balfour Declaration was largely a "public relations exercise" to mobilize international Jewish support and the agreement of the United States and France to British control of Palestine after the war. So there was every advantage to Britain in publishing the declaration (except in Palestine itself, where the British military administration feared that it would provoke disturbances).

Finally, whereas the Husayn-McMahon exchange was inconclusive and never resulted in any form of agreement signed by representatives of either side, the Balfour Declaration was a unilateral statement of intent by the British foreign secretary on behalf of the British cabinet. This is not to detract from the moral value of either document, if indeed international relations do have a moral dimension. It is merely to state the obvious difference between a proposal in an exchange of letters that was never ratified by the British cabinet, much less agreed to by Husayn himself, and a unilateral statement of British intent toward the Jews, a public document that later was incorporated in the League of Nations mandate over Palestine and thereby became part and parcel of the international obligations Britain undertook in accepting the mandate.

The neutral observer might make a case that both undertakings were equally binding on the British. One might also claim, as Arabs have, that if the two undertakings were found to be mutually exclusive, then the earlier must take precedence over the later. One might in fact question the right of the British to make commitments regarding Ottoman territory to any third party. However, once both Arabs and Jews chose to base their claims to Palestine even partially on British wartime undertakings, each side rendered itself vulnerable to changing British interpretations of their own interests. As Machiavelli pointed out so long ago, politics are not conducted according to the precepts of private morality.

CHAPTER THREE

Mandatory Problems,
1920–1945

Britain's Middle Eastern Empire

With the accretions won by military conquest during the war, the British empire reached its apogee. In the Middle East Britain assumed control of vast expanses of territory hitherto ruled loosely by the Turks.

Even prior to the war, however, British statesmen had reached a consensus that "further extensions to the formal empire were more likely to weaken than to strengthen the foundations of British world power."[1] The huge costs of the war had sapped confidence even further and created a new sense of imperial vulnerability. It was now clear that the economic foundations upon which the empire had been acquired and maintained during the eighteenth and nineteenth centuries would be unable to sustain any further expansion. In addition, the Lloyd George coalition faced intense domestic pressures after the war, both financial

1. John Darwin, *Britain, Egypt, and the Middle East: Imperial Policy in the Aftermath of War, 1918–1922* (London, 1981), p. 8; this volume treats British imperial policy in the Middle East after World War I in admirable detail.

and political. In the face of demands to demobilize and reduce overseas expenditure, the cabinet accepted without
formal debate Lloyd George's proposal that the army be
cut back to the pre-1914 levels. The military's estimates of
the troop strengths that would be required to hold on
to the new empire were dismissed out of hand. The new
territories in the Middle East presented especially acute
problems: although racked by nascent, yet turbulent, nationalist movements, they seemed to be deficient in taxable
commodities. The contrast between the troublesome "New
Provinces" in the Middle East and the traditional empire in
black Africa was drawn in colorful terms by the colonial
secretary, Sir Winston Churchill, during a debate in the
House of Commons on 14 July 1921:

> In the Middle East you have arid countries. In East
> Africa you have dripping countries. There is the great-
> est difficulty to get anything to grow in one place, and
> the greatest difficulty to prevent things smothering
> and choking you by their hurried growth in the other.
> In the African colonies you have a docile, tractable
> population, who only require to be well and wisely
> treated to develop great economic capacity and util-
> ity; whereas the regions of the Middle East are unduly
> stocked with peppery, pugnacious and proud politi-
> cians and theologians, who happen to be at the same
> time extremely well armed and extremely hard up.[2]

After World War I, Winston Churchill played a major
role in the determination of Britain's Middle Eastern policy,
first as secretary of state for war and air (1919—1921), and

2. Churchill, Speech to the House of Commons, 14 July 1921, *Parliamentary Debates* (Commons), 5th ser., vol. 144, col. 1626. This and
other extracts quoted from Churchill's writings and speeches may also
be found in Michael J. Cohen, *Churchill and the Jews* (London, 1985).

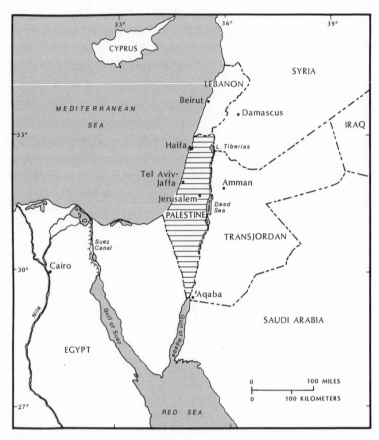

Map 3. The Palestine Mandate, 1920–1948

then as secretary of state for the colonies (1921–1922). Both departments disposed of huge budgets by prewar standards, and both were therefore under pressure to reduce and retrench. At the War Office in particular, Churchill was perturbed that his department was spending exorbitant amounts to maintain a huge standing army in the Middle East implementing policies determined by other departments—and this at a time when the public was concerned more to reduce unemployment at home than to dissipate resources in overseas extravagances. Churchill was inspired and guided by the vigorous chief of the imperial general staff, Field Marshal Sir Henry Wilson, whose contempt for the dithering and lack of judgment displayed by the politicians ("the frocks," he called them) found expression in his constant scathing attacks on the irresponsible dispersion of Britain's reduced forces across the expanses of the Middle East.

The War Office, with Churchill at its head, wanted to relinquish the "New Provinces" of the Middle East and return them to their former Turkish masters. In a series of private letters to Prime Minister Lloyd George, Churchill argued that Britain, France, and Greece should all give up their Middle Eastern possessions. This was a policy Churchill continued to press from the Colonial Office. Churchill and many of his colleages in the cabinet were concerned that Kemal Atatürk would lead a war of revenge against the Allies and, perhaps with the aid of the Bolsheviks, sweep down on the Middle East and retake it by force. Thus in mid-1921, with the Palestine mandate yet to be ratified by the League of Nations (owing to American and French objections), Churchill penned the following letter to Lloyd George:

I now learn that the League of Nations wish to postpone the Mandates for Palestine and Mesopotamia
until the Americans are satisfied, i.e., indefinite postponement. I ought to warn you that if this course is
followed and if at the same time the Turkish situation
degenerates in a disastrous manner, it will be impossible for us to maintain our position either in Palestine or in Mesopotamia, and the only wise and safe
course would be to take advantage of the postponement of the Mandates and resign them both and quit
the two countries at the earliest possible moment, as
the expense to which we shall be put will be wholly
unwarrantable.[3]

But Lloyd George's Middle Eastern policy was determined by wider considerations. He was determined to restrict "Ottoman imperialism" to Anatolia. In his view, and
that of Foreign Secretary Curzon, any British withdrawal
from the Middle East would pave the way for a revival of
the degenerate Ottoman empire, with the consequent loss
of British war gains and thus an incalculable loss of status
and prestige.

John Darwin has concluded that Palestine itself was "peripheral" to the main objects of imperial expansion after
World War I and that the British presence in Palestine was
strategically and politically a pendant of their operations
elsewhere. This view would seem to underestimate the strategic importance attributed to Palestine by British policy-
makers after the war, as shown in two significant illustra-
tions. First, note the interesting case of Curzon, who in
1917 had opposed the issue of the Balfour Declaration to

3. Churchill to Lloyd George, 2 June 1921, quoted in Cohen,
Churchill and the Jews, p. 96.

the Zionists but in 1923 gave the following post factum justification for Britain's tenure in Palestine:

> We cannot now recede. If we did the French would step in and then be on the threshold of Egypt and on the outskirts of the [Suez] Canal. Besides Palestine needed ports, electricity, and the Jews of America were rich and would subsidise such development.[4]

Compare that statement to this opinion, expressed in a cabinet memorandum dated March 1928 by none other than Balfour himself, the eponym, even if not the author, of the 1917 declaration:

> Palestine . . . lies at the very place where the Power primarily responsible for the security of the Suez Canal would wish to place it. . . . A mandated territory on the Asiatic side of the great waterway, prosperous, contented and quite impervious to Egyptian intrigue must add strength to the Empire at a point where additional strength may in the interests of the Empire and the world, be most desirable. This was not a consideration which influenced most British Zionists in 1917. It certainly did not influence me; but the trend of events since then has brought it into prominence, and the idealists—be they Jew or Gentile are serving the interests of peace and commerce in a way which perhaps they never contemplated.[5]

Britain's Quest for Legitimacy

In the Middle East, a new term was coined to accommodate "enlightened" colonialism to Wilsonian principles

4. Quoted in *Thomas Jones, Whitehall Diary,* vol. 1: *1916–1925,* ed. Keith Middlemass (London, 1969), p. 246.

5. Cabinet memorandum, CP 71, 5 March 1928, Cab. 24/193.

of self-determination. The new international agency, the
League of Nations, was to allot "mandates," or international trusteeships, under which the powers were to prepare peoples liberated from the Turks for independence.
The mandates were intended to be self-terminating once
the indigenous peoples had matured sufficiently to "jus-
tify" their independence. It must remain doubtful whether
in fact this moral instrument influenced British policy in
Palestine to any extent. However, the necessity of submit-
ting the constitutional arrangements for mandatory control to the league's council—where they might be chal-
lenged by France or, indirectly, by the United States—may
have acted as a deterrent to more blatantly imperialist
policies.

But once the United States abdicated any further role in
the new European order after the summer of 1919, it was
left to Britain and France to divide the Middle East between them. It cannot be said that either power displayed
any great altruism when it came to deciding whether the
indigenous peoples of the area were mature enough to be
granted their independence.

In April 1920, in the small Italian town of San Remo,
Britain and France divided the Middle East into mandates
while the American ambassador read his newspaper in the
garden. Britain obtained Palestine, Transjordan,[6] and Iraq;
the French acquired Syria. Both countries had to crush

6. Palestine and Transjordan remained a single administrative unit
until 1946, but in 1922 Transjordan was detached from the area to
which the Balfour Declaration applied. This has remained a grievance
with the Zionist side, but it should be remembered that the area to the
east of the river Jordan was definitely included in the area promised to
Husayn in 1915; the linking of Palestine and Transjordan had been an
administrative convenience for Britain and did not indicate any recognition of Zionist claims to the East Bank of the Jordan.

rebellions against the mandatory system that summer—
France in Syria, in the course of which the Hashemite regime was dismantled and Faysal sent packing; and Britain,
a long and costly rebellion in Iraq. In Palestine, Britain had
to cope with Arab disturbances in March 1920 and May
1921 in protest against its "Zionist" policy.

Winston Churchill appreciated soon enough that Britain
was precluded from granting the Arabs any unrestricted
form of self-government by British obligations to the Jews
under the Balfour Declaration, which was itself incorporated into the League of Nations mandate. From the out-
set the Arabs protested the growth of the Jewish national
home in Palestine, and it was perfectly apparent that given
the slightest chance the indigenous Arab majority would
legislate a stoppage of Jewish immigration and land purchases—which the Balfour Declaration required Britain to
facilitate.

The first British high commissioner, Sir Herbert Samuel,
tried by many methods to persuade the Palestinians to participate in the process of government, but he was rebuffed
each time. Samuel put forward numerous proposals for
granting self-rule to the Arabs, from advisory to legislative
councils, to the idea of an Arab agency that would parallel
the Jewish Agency constituted by the Zionist Organization.
All were rejected by the Arab leadership, which via the me-
dium of the Supreme Muslim Council was able to enforce
a boycott of the elections arranged by Samuel. With the
failure of the various constitutional schemes, the administration fell back on recruiting Arabs to the civil service as
a way of obtaining the community's de facto allegiance.
The Arabs' rejection of the government's legislative council scheme left them without any constitutional forum in
which to air their grievances or acquire the arts of self-

rule. But for the Arabs, official posts were primarily a means of personal advancement and gain, in contrast to the Jews, for whom appointments symbolized recognition of their community and legitimation of their national aspirations. With both communities, however, first loyalties were reserved for their own people. In this sense, the Palestine mandate, as a political entity, was from the first a fiction.

The British could never offer the degree of legislative independence demanded by the Arabs, who maintained the public stance that acceptance of positions in British constitutional instruments would signify recognition of the mandatory regime. The Arabs consistently denied the legality of that regime, and so from the beginning the British failed to secure the allegiance, or even the acquiescence, of the majority of the people they had come to rule.

In 1922 the British issued the first of several white papers that attempted to define and explain their policy in Palestine, in effect to clarify the meaning and intent of the Balfour Declaration. The British government reassured the Arabs that whereas the Jews were in Palestine "as of right, and not on sufferance," it had never been the government's intention to impose a Jewish majority on the Arabs. But the exaggerated hopes and fears of each community were not to be dissipated that easily. In Palestine itself, the status of the Jewish community had been transformed from that of aliens, who had been tolerated, and at times expelled, by the Turkish regime, to that of first-class citizens, officially recognized and sponsored by the British regime. Moreover, for the brief period from 1937 to 1938, when Britain was considering the partition of Palestine into Arab and Jewish states, it seemed that those hopes and fears had not been so exaggerated after all.

Many Jews had regarded the Balfour Declaration as sig-

nifying the coming of the millennium. But bitter disappoint-
ments and disillusionment were in store. The first high commissioner, a Jew, did not live up to their expectations. But
neither did the Jewish people as a whole respond adequately to the opportunity afforded by the political breakthrough. The Jews thought that Samuel had betrayed their
cause when he suspended Jewish immigration following
the May riots in 1921 (see pp. 80−81).

But the Jews were prepared to swallow many bitter pills
in order to gain more time in which to establish themselves
as an immovable entity in Palestine. It was only in 1939,
when the British signaled a definite stop to the further development of the Jewish national home, that the Jews too
withdrew their allegiance from the British regime.

The Palestinian Arabs:
Political and Socioeconomic Upheaval

To simplify a complex issue, one might say that Palestinian
Arab nationalism was ignited by two major processes after
World War I: first, by the division of Ottoman Syria into
mandates by France and Britain; second, by the British
promotion of Zionism in Palestine.

Initially, Palestinian political activity after the war had
focused on Damascus. Palestinian Arabs held important
positions in Faysal's administration there, and most radical
Palestinian activists worked toward the goal of a greater
Syria under Faysal's rule. A Palestinian Arab delegation that
wished to give evidence to this effect at the Paris peace conference was prevented from traveling by the British, who
were set on dividing greater Syria with the French and ruling Palestine themselves. When Faysal was deposed by the
French in July 1920, the Palestinians had to give up their
hopes of a greater Syria and return home to Palestine to

tackle their own local problems. The first two Palestinian national congresses had been held in Damascus, but significantly the third, in December 1920, was held in Haifa.

Since the British conquest of Palestine in 1918, the country had been ruled by General Allenby's military administration. The British army wished above all else to maintain peace and stability in the area under its control. The military had not been privy to the varied motives that had prompted the Balfour Declaration, and they now warned the government in London that pursuit of that policy would provoke the Palestinians to revolt, jeopardizing the British position in the entire region. At the army's insistence the text of the Balfour Declaration was not published in Palestine itself until after the San Remo conference.

The first violent Palestinian protest against Britain's policy came in March 1920, at the same time that Faysal was crowned king of greater Syria by the national congress at Damascus. The military administration in Palestine recommended that Faysal be nominated ruler of Palestine and that the Balfour pledge be rescinded. There is some circumstantial evidence that the army turned a blind eye to the 1920 disturbances in order to be able to support its own recommendations with a demonstration of Arab force.

The government in London, however, remained that which had issued the Balfour Declaration. For Lloyd George, the pledge to the Zionists not only was a matter of national honor but it also provided the raison d'être and international legitimation of British rule in Palestine, a strategic asset to the north of the Suez Canal. Instead of conceding to the army's demands, then, in July 1920 London replaced the military administration with a civil government.

Sir Herbert Samuel granted amnesty to those implicated in the disturbances of the previous March and embarked on a policy of alliances with the traditional ruling elites in the Arab community. The two leading families, the Husaynis and the Nashashibis, were the main recipients of British largesse. British policy was one of "personal rewards coupled with institutional changes that made the positions of their allies within the indigenous community seemingly inviolable."[7]

The Husayni family in particular was given a plethora of offices and titles without precedent in Palestinian history. Kamil al-Husayni, a leading scion of the family, and mufti of Jerusalem, was rewarded for his early cooperation with the regime by being elevated to an unheard-of combination of powerful religious positions, becoming head of the Central Waqf Committee and president of the Shariʿa court of appeal in Jerusalem. (Shariʿa means the revealed Holy Law of Islam.) In addition, the British secured for him the new title of grand mufti, which gave the Husaynis and the city of Jerusalem an unprecedented preeminent position in Palestine's Muslim community. After Kamil's death in 1921, the British sponsored the meteoric rise to prominence of a younger member of the clan, Haj Amin al-Husayni. Amin was given amnesty by Samuel for his role in inciting the riots of March 1920 and, on promise of good behavior, was maneuvered by the British into the office of grand mufti (he had won only fourth position in the primary elections).[8] Seeing that the Husayni mayor of Jerusalem had been dismissed for his part in the 1920 riots, Samuel's policy of balancing between the two leading families dictated

7. Joel S. Migdal, ed., *Palestinian Society and Politics* (Princeton, N.J., 1980), p. 20.

8. On the election of Haj Amin al-Husayni, see Elie Kedourie, "Sir Herbert Samuel and the Government of Palestine," *Middle Eastern Studies* 5 (January 1969): 44–68.

that a Husayni obtain the office of mufti. In 1922 Haj Amin was also appointed president of the newly constituted Supreme Muslim Council (SMC), which was given wide powers and discretion over the disbursement of considerable funds (from religious endowments, fees, and so on).

The new institutions served as agencies for the growth of a political and religious leadership replacing that previously exercised by the Turks from Constantinople. The SMC, whose income rose from £50,000 in 1921 to £62,000 in 1931, commanded a vast patronage of religious positions, for the restoration of mosques, the construction of schools, and various grants that could be offered as rewards to Husayni supporters or denied to their opponents. The SMC constituted the only agency of Palestinian self-rule, yet it was never subjected to the normal processes of democratic selection. The president, Haj Amin al-Husayni, evaded the constitutional obligation to stand for reelection, thus depriving his political opponents of any orderly means of unseating him.

Samuel's policy achieved concrete short-term success. From 1922 to 1929 there was relative peace and stability in Palestine. But in the long term the policy of alliances with notables, in particular with the Husayni family, had drastic consequences for all parties concerned—the British, the Zionists, and the Palestinians themselves. Haj Amin al-Husayni was able eventually to dictate Palestinian politics, denying all expression to alternative views. The royal commission sent out by the British government in 1936 to investigate the causes of the Arab rebellion of that year drew attention to the anomalous position attained by the SMC, which, it asserted, had become an "*imperium in imperio.*" The British administration was censured severely for having allowed such a state of affairs to come to pass.

The British policy of alliances with the traditional elite had a certain stabilizing effect on the Arab community in Palestine, at least for the first half of the mandatory period. Via the patronage at its command, the Husayni clan was able to tie even the smallest villages into a network of political allegiance. Leaders in small villages attached their clans to those in larger ones, and the latter were attached directly to major city families. A similar pyramidal structure linked the opposition clans and their supporters.

At the same time, however, major social and economic transformations were eroding traditional, predominantly agrarian, Palestinian society. The imposition of British rule in Palestine, with its novel bureaucratic methods and the support it gave to the predominantly European Jewish influx, drastically affected the Arabs' traditional ties of family and religion. These ties had provided an important sense of security, based on attachments both to notable groups and to the larger Ottoman empire, seat of the Muslim caliphate. Unlike the Ottoman regime, the elements of Western society and administration now grafted onto Palestine were alien both in culture and in religion. The gap between Arab and Jewish levels of literacy, living standards, and economic power inevitably had repercussions on political developments within the Arab community. Many Arabs came to believe that autonomy would come only with control over an independent national state, a belief reinforced by the growth of Jewish quasi-governmental institutions.

Officials of the mandatory government used unfamiliar standards of justice and sought to regulate village relationships in accordance with their own view of stability. In so doing, they inevitably weakened traditional structures without providing acceptable substitutes. The revolt of 1936–1939 reflected, and further exacerbated, the disorder and destitution that engulfed much of rural Palestine during the 1930s. The coincidence of a growing nationalist movement with the fragmentation of village society created the illusion of a unified movement against the mandate. Foreign control over the state at times obscured the nature of the problems faced. Throughout the mandatory period Palestinian Arabs remained divided against themselves, struggling to cope with developments they either failed to comprehend or felt they had little control over.[9]

One of the most fundamental of these problems was that of land ownership. The Palestinian peasants' principal means of livelihood was also both the basis of the Arab notables' traditional leadership and the key to the Zionists' colonizing success. Until the publication of a recent in-depth study of the land problem by Kenneth W. Stein,[10] this particular aspect of the Palestine conflict was usually overshadowed by the more obvious manifestation of the Zionist enterprise, immigration. Studies that have touched on the problem have reserved their indictments primarily for the Zionists and secondarily for the British. The Arab leaders' own complicity has been largely ignored or overlooked.

There were several subjective reasons why the land question was given such a low profile for so long. Britain itself, being unable or perhaps unwilling to control the economic

9. On the social upheavals caused by the British mandate, see Ylana N. Miller, "Administrative Policy in Rural Palestine: The Impact of British Norms on Arab Community Life, 1920–1948," in Migdal, *Palestinian Society and Politics*. For details and statistics pertaining to levels of literacy, population growth, and health indices, see also Ann Mosely Lesch, *Arab Politics in Palestine, 1917–1939* (Ithaca, N.Y., 1979), chap. 3.

10. Kenneth W. Stein, *The Land Question in Palestine, 1917–1939* (Chapel Hill, N.C., 1984).

forces that ruled the land market, placed greater emphasis on the problem of immigration. In addition, and significantly, Arab leaders themselves were at all periods, even at the height of the conflict, personally and profitably involved in the land market. The rising land values that Zionist demand engendered enabled the effendi (landowning) class to maintain a certain life-style and status so long as they were permitted to manipulate the market at will, which they did in full collaboration with the Jews. During the 1930s, a period of severe economic depression, sales of land to Jews enabled a class of impoverished or bankrupt small landowners to stay afloat. The Zionists themselves were extremely discreet about the prominent Arabs with whom they traded; they kept their own confidential lists of those engaged in the land market and deliberately withheld names from British commissions of inquiry so as not to jeopardize future sales.

In fact, the British had their own sources of information and were fully apprised of the nature and scale of land transactions. They "carefully guarded the prestige of the landowning class by never publicly faulting it for collaborating with the Jews in land sales."[11] The British relied heavily on imported Jewish capital, not only to fuel the economy but also to pay for the Jewish community's social services and, so long as security expenditure could be kept down during tranquil periods, to keep the Palestine budget in healthy surplus. In 1928 the Yishuv (Hebrew, "settle-

11. Ibid., p. 30. Stein, who painstakingly worked through the British administration's land registration and Lands Department files, provides a twelve-page appendix listing Palestinian leaders who engaged in land sales to the Jews, whether as sellers, brokers, or agents. The list includes all the prominent Palestinian Arab families, from the Husaynis, Nashashibis, and al-Hadis to Musa al-Alami himself.

ment": the Jewish community in Palestine), which com-
prised some 17 percent of the total population, contributed
44 percent of the government's revenue.

The British appreciated that any restriction of land sales
would probably inhibit Jewish immigration and the capital
that came with it. Jewish capital was all the more essential
because the British themselves were parsimonious toward
Palestine and unwilling to bail out the Palestinian peasantry, large parts of which were reduced to penury during
the 1930s. In 1930 a British land expert, Sir John Hope-
Simpson, estimated that no further arable land reserves remained in Palestine and suggested that all further sales to
Jews should be prohibited. But his report also included a
development plan that required the investment of £7.2 million. The British government, beset by the Great Depression of 1929, the effects of which were spreading through
Europe, reduced the amount first to £2.5 million, and then
to £500,000. Eventually, a mere £84,000 was spent, mostly
on the resettlement of landless Arabs. No effort was made,
or money spent, to reform Arab agricultural methods.

In the Arab sector, over 25 percent of the Muslim population eked out less than a subsistence living from the land.
Primitive methods yielded poor results, and on top of this a
series of natural and climatic disasters—drought, field mice,
locusts, even an earthquake—exacerbated the situation. In
the 1930s worldwide overproduction of cereals and their
consequent dumping in Palestine caused a further drop in
local prices, reducing still further any profit the Arab peasants might in normal circumstances have expected to wring
from their plots. Thus, during the 1930s the Arab peasants' inability to pay their tithes to the government or their
mortgage debts to their Arab landlords forced more and

more small tenants to sell off their lands, notwithstanding the increasingly anti-Zionist political climate.

It should be noted also that although Arab poverty was undoubtedly a principal motive behind land sales to Jews, it was not the only one. There were equally many Arabs, especially absentee landlords, who, although economically solvent, engaged in sales to Jews for sheer profit. The army of brokers and agents who acted as intermediaries in order to protect the identity of the sellers were similarly motivated.

The major turning point came in the 1930s. Until then Jewish land purchases had concentrated on large, uncultivated, often untenanted areas owned by absentee landlords. But with the worsening economic conditions in the 1930s, more and more indigenous small owners and cultivators were reduced to penury and forced to capitalize on at least a part of their holdings. Stein has calculated that between 1932 and 1945 some 65 percent of all land bought by Jews came from resident Palestinians. The scale of these sales at last aroused the Palestinian Arab leadership, which resolved to investigate the transactions of its own members, but it is highly doubtful whether any concerted measures were ever taken. A conspiracy of silence persisted, and sales continued.

Nothing served more to convince the Zionists that Arab political opposition was insincere and artificial. They realized that official restrictions and regulations could always be circumvented, no matter how strident the Arabs' public protests. The only objective obstacle to land purchase was the Jews' own dearth of capital. No British legislation could ever "protect" the Arabs against their own landowners' determination to profit from an ever-rising market; to the contrary, each time the British announced new legislation, the Zionists were overwhelmed with offers of land from Arabs keen to preempt the new measures to "protect" them. With their paternalistic, yet parsimonious policies, the British increasingly blamed the Zionists for unsettled conditions in Palestine, thus diverting attention from their own frugality and the Arab effendis' own collusion in the sales. But a thorough reform of the Arab agrarian economy, enough to have made it at least self-sufficient, would likely have required an investment far beyond that which any colonial power was willing to make.

Some effort was exerted by Arab leaders to stem the tide of land sales to Jews.[12] Sporadic attempts were made to buy up lands, to take court action to prevent sales, to establish banks and funds for long-term loans, and to convince farmers to hold on to their plots, all without significant success. Not only were such attempts undermined by the clandestine unofficial market, about which few spoke in public, but total assets available for land redemption were also pitifully low. In 1929 total Arab bank deposits amounted to only £376,000. In January 1935 Haj Amin al-Husayni convened a conference of 509 learned *ulama* (religious scholars, jurists, teachers, and dignitaries—the Islamic "priesthood") which endorsed a *fatwa* (religious edict) against land sales and land brokerage. The conference threatened to excommunicate all those who sold their lands or acted as brokers for such transactions.

But any effort to inhibit the land market was caught in an ironic vicious circle. Most Arab capital assets were in property, and the very funds needed to preempt further sales to the Jews could have been raised only by selling off

12. On these efforts, see Lesch, *Arab Politics,* pp. 67–74. Note that Lesch does not mention the complicity of the Arab leaders themselves.

land, thereby defeating the very purpose of the transaction. The Palestinian Arabs themselves possessed neither the required degree of national cohesion nor the institutions with which they might have withstood the lure of quick, even if ephemeral, riches.

In contrast to the depressed agrarian sector of the Arab economy, great prosperity was brought to Palestine by extensive capital imported by both the British and the Jews. British investment undermined the monopolistic control of the traditional Arab elite and attenuated the extent of the peasantry's dependence on it. Ironically, the effendis' sales of their tenants' lands also contributed to the rupture of feudal land links, as the peasants became urbanized manual laborers. Jewish capital did not go only to Arab landlords; probably well over half of it went directly into the Arab economy as rents and in payment for agricultural produce, services, and materials. British investment increased substantially during World War II, when huge British armies straddled the Middle East and consumed huge quantities of supplies.

During the 1930s the depression in Arab agriculture drew Arabs westward from the hilly inland areas to more lucrative employment in the urban centers along the coast. Jerusalem, which in 1922 had housed the largest percentage of the total Arab population (38 percent), was during the 1930s overtaken by Haifa, whose Arab population had grown from 25 to 33 percent of the total; at the same time, Jerusalem's share fell to 26 percent. Counter-elites thus grew up in Jaffa and in Haifa, where the traditional elites were weakest (both the Husayni and the Nashashibi families were based in Jerusalem). As the center of gravity in the country moved from Jerusalem to the coastal plain, more and more of those who prospered sought roles in the host of new institutions there. But no direct challenge to the old families was mounted, for most of the new institutions were economic (banks, chambers of commerce) and social rather than political in character.

But new economic resources and new prosperity for some did not bring social integration to the Palestinian Arabs. The politics of intimidation and retaliation that so marked the latter stages of the Arab revolt (from 1936 to 1939; see below) was unleashed after 1945 with great self-destruction owing to the social fragmentation that had been accelerated by developments during World War II. As summed up by Joel S. Migdal, "assassination and threat of assassination characterized the political climate of those last few critical years before 1948." Thus, at the most critical moment in their history, during their struggle for independence, "the Palestinians found themselves without a strong, dominant class to lead them, without leadership capable of mobilizing them into an effective political or military force."[13]

The Zionists' Progress

The progress of the Jewish national home was characterized by naive expectations, disillusionment with its British patrons, and a proclivity for factionalism and internal division that hampered the Zionist effort, not only in Palestine itself but also in the Diaspora.

Following the achievement of the Balfour Declaration, leadership of the Zionist movement had come to rest quite naturally with Chaim Weizmann, who received major credit for the breakthrough. Since all major decisions regarding Palestine now rested with the British government, it was

13. Migdal, *Palestinian Society and Politics,* p. 31.

also natural that the political headquarters of the Zionist movement should be in London, under Weizmann's direction. But this led to a somewhat anomalous situation. Those actually doing the colonizing in Palestine were building up a new community with its own particular ideological and social environment, while supreme political control rested with men living in a totally different environment thousands of miles away. The real and imagined opposition of the British administration to the Yishuv only encouraged this "division of authority." Because the Jews in Palestine were often unable to secure their demands from a hostile officialdom, they resorted to going over those officials' heads to London, where Weizmann's personal charm and influence with the establishment proved to be an indispensable asset.

The physical distance between political headquarters and "the field" produced mental and social divisions that caused frictions, misunderstandings, and eventually a power struggle between the two. The community in Palestine obtained full sovereign control only with the establishment of the state of Israel in 1948, and its support by Diaspora Jewry has remained a critical factor in Israel's survival ever since.

The Zionist movement was itself critically divided after the war. A rift soon emerged between the traditional European-based cadres and the leaders of the movement in North America. Judge Louis Brandeis, Supreme Court justice and head of the American Zionist movement, believed that the political era of Zionism had ended with the Balfour Declaration. All that remained, in his opinion, was to develop Palestine's economic potential and absorb the new immigrants. Because he believed that the world Zionist movement's political functions were complete, Brandeis

advocated the establishment of national federations tied
loosely to the center. He objected to a single national fund
that might hinder investments for specific purposes, but he
did agree to a central fund into which donations, though
not investments, might be channeled. In the clash that developed between Weizmann and Brandeis after the war, it
seems that there was a large element of personal difference
and rivalry for the leadership of the movement.

Weizmann and his group believed that Brandeis's "de-
centralizing" schemes would affect the very essence and
character of the movement, not to mention the authority of
the central office, then in London. Weizmann was too per-
spicacious to believe that the political struggle was over—
he was still engaged in a struggle to determine the borders
of the mandate. More than that, Weizmann saw the movement as representing the national will for liberation, not
merely as an economic enterprise run on orthodox business principles. Weizmann eventually emerged supreme,
defeating Brandeis on his home ground at a convention of
American Zionists held in Cleveland in 1921. But the price
was heavy, in more senses than one. Brandeis and his group
left the movement, and American Zionism entered a depression that lasted until the late 1930s. During the period
between the two world wars, American Jewry gave for relief of European Jews fifteen times the amount they gave to
the Yishuv.

Financial weakness and the sealing off of Soviet Jewry by
the Bolsheviks were perhaps the two most significant factors that affected the Yishuv in the 1920s. Economic difficulties coupled with inability to absorb those immigrants
who did reach Palestine became a political handicap. In
May 1921 a street fight between rival Jewish radical factions on the Tel Aviv–Jaffa border developed into a fight

with the Arabs and led to general Arab rioting against the Jews. The Jewish population of Jaffa bore the brunt of Arab hostility. The immigration-hostel, the first stop of all new Jewish immigrants, was burned to the ground, and some forty-three Jews were either burned or shot to death. Lord Samuel saw these acts as symbolizing Arab opposition to Jewish immigration, to which he ordered an immediate suspension.

The 1921 riots caused a radical change in Samuel's attitude to Zionism. He was now convinced that the Zionists, unable in any case to achieve a quick majority in Palestine and to convert it into a Jewish state, would henceforth have to proceed at a more gradual pace to avoid future Arab hostility. Samuel was influenced also by his intimate knowledge of Zionist weakness. What was the point in maximal political goals which the Jews were unable to live up to in reality?

Not only had the Zionists proved unable to take advantage of all the immigration certificates Samuel had authorized (16,500, for that many heads of families), but they had also had to discourage their branches in Europe from sending more people. When this action failed to stem the tide, the Zionist office in London had to ask the Foreign Office to curtail the number of visas it issued for Palestine.[14]

Thus, on the occasion of the riots of May 1921 Samuel believed he might at one and the same time appease the Arabs and relieve the pressure on the Zionists' limited resources. But Samuel's decision lacked political acumen. The timing was bad, creating the impression that Britain could be forced by Arab violence to retreat from its com-

14. See Moshe Mossek, *The Immigration Policy of Sir Herbert Samuel* (London, 1979).

mitment to Zionism. Samuel claimed in vain that he had done the Zionists a favor, that had he not suspended immigration they themselves would have been forced to ask him to do so. Samuel's name became anathema to the Zionists, yet his very Jewishness prevented them from asking for his removal as some radicals suggested.

Immigration was soon renewed, but the numbers who actually arrived were not significantly higher than in previous years. Moreover, the Zionists' financial troubles persisted. "There is no money, no work, and there can be no immigration," the British head of the Zionist commission in Palestine wrote in March 1922. Yet of far greater long-term significance was the new policy that Samuel pressed on London after the 1921 riots, a policy eventually promulgated in July 1922 as a white paper.

This document, mistakenly known as the "Churchill White Paper," was the first attempt by London to define British commitments to Jews and Arabs and above all to clarify what the Balfour Declaration had really meant. (The real authors of the new policy were the high commissioner, Samuel, and Sir John Shuckburgh, head of the Colonial Office's Eastern Department.) Its principles guided British policy in Palestine until 1939. Its goal, impossible to achieve, was to reassure and placate each community concerning its own security and future in Palestine.

The Jews were reassured that they were in Palestine "as of right, and not on sufferance." The Arabs were reassured in their turn that the British government had no intention of imposing a Jewish state in Palestine and that the further development of the Jewish national home would not mean "the imposition of a Jewish nationality upon the inhabitants of Palestine as a whole." The white paper also proposed the establishment of a legislative council, but, as we have already seen, the Arab community, led by the SMC, boycotted the elections to this body.

The white paper's most far-reaching practical proposal lay in the unprecedented regulations it laid down regarding immigration. Henceforth, immigration would not be allowed to exceed what the British considered to be the "economic absorptive capacity" of Palestine. New immigrants would not be allowed to become a burden on the British taxpayer or to deprive any Palestinians of their jobs. In 1922 this measure reflected economic reality. During the 1930s, however, when Jewish immigration soared, the formula could be used by officialdom arbitrarily for political purposes. In 1937 the Peel Commission stated for the first time that the volume of immigration could no longer be determined solely according to economic criteria but must be treated as a political issue, one that was arousing Arab fears and animosity. When the commission proposed the partition of Palestine into Arab and Jewish states, it also proposed that further Jewish immigration should in the interim be restricted to a "political high level."

The economic criteria laid down in 1922 promoted one further development. They added a pragmatic and patriotic motive to the socialist Zionist policy of creating a normal Jewish working class in Palestine. Now the Histadrut labor union would argue with Jewish employers who hired cheaper, and usually more efficient, Arab labor that each job given to a Jew (instead of to an Arab) would permit the entry of one more Jewish immigrant family to help build up the national home. The Jewish working class was thus able to identify its own cause with that of the nation. But in the process many Jewish socialists were forced to make a painful choice between class solidarity with their Arab fellow workers and their patriotic duty to the national home.

Crossroads in the 1930s

The calm that settled on Palestine after the 1921 riots had spread a general attitude of complacency. British forces in Palestine had by 1919 been run down to a total of 292 police in the entire country, supplemented of course by local supernumeraries. In the summer of 1929 High Commissioner Sir John Chancellor (appointed only the previous January) was on leave in London. He and Colonial Office officials complimented one another on the fact that Palestine was "an island of peace." The Zionist leadership had decamped to Europe en bloc to attend the Sixteenth Zionist Congress. Neither the British nor the Zionists suspected that the troubles that had been brewing for over a year over access by Jews and Arabs to the Wailing Wall in Jerusalem were about to erupt into the bloodiest Arab riots Palestine had yet witnessed.

The circumstances of the 1929 disturbances and the factors that touched them off remain clouded and a matter for continuing debate among historians.[15] One of the mufti's own associates, Izzat Darwaza (a supervisor of the Muslim Waqf, or religious endowments, at the time), has since written that the mufti himself incited the masses to action in order to reassert his own position as a popular leader following his loss of ground to the Nashashibi opposition, particularly during the 1927 municipal elections. The issue chosen was the longstanding dispute over Jewish rights to worship at the Western, or Wailing, Wall. Jewish claims to unrestricted worship were contested by the Arabs, who re-

15. The latest thesis on the disturbances, which denies the mufti's association with the riots, is found in Philip Mattar's "The Mufti's Role in the Disturbances at the Wailing Wall, 1928–29," *Middle Eastern Studies* 19 (January 1983):104–118.

garded the same wall (called by them al-Buraq) as sacred, the Prophet Muhammad reportedly having tied his horse to it before ascending to Heaven. It seems that large sections of the Arab community genuinely came to believe in a Jewish conspiracy to take over this particular holy place.

In addition, the Arabs may have been concerned by new developments within the Zionist movement. The Zionist effort in Palestine had reached the depths of depression during the last years of the decade. An acute economic crisis had resulted in mass emigration, and in 1928 more Jews left Palestine than arrived. In 1929, however, the Zionist congress decided on the establishment of an enlarged Jewish Agency, whose goal would be to mobilize the resources of American Jewry to renew and stimulate Zionist growth. In addition, the revisionist leader Ze'ev Jabotinsky may have alarmed the Arabs with his demand, made in the congress plenum, that the movement declare as its final goal the establishment of a Jewish state in Palestine. (The demand was in fact rejected by the congress, and Jabotinsky led his party out of the Zionist movement.) There appears to be little doubt that the events at the Zionist congress, together with certain provocations in Jerusalem itself, sparked the disturbances, in places pogroms, that now swept Palestine.

The riots began on 23 August in Jerusalem and during the course of the next week spread to the whole of Palestine. Britain rushed in reinforcements by rail and air and dispatched five warships to Palestinian coastal waters. The worst single incident occurred at Hebron, where over sixty of the traditional orthodox community were slaughtered in a pogrom reminiscent of tsarist Russia. Many Jewish settlements, including Hebron, were abandoned by the Jews, who would return only after the 1967 war. Jews in charge of security learned the bitter lesson that their forces had to be organized on a national scale rather than for local regional defense, the pattern hitherto.

As had become the tradition in Palestine, a commission of inquiry was set up to establish the causes of the disturbances. The Shaw Commission report, dated March 1930, concluded that the 1929 riots had been neither premeditated by the Arabs nor provoked by the Jews. The immediate provocation over the Wailing Wall was relegated to the background, and the commission focused on Arab fears and disappointment with respect to the attainment of their national goals. The Jews' policy of excluding Arab labor from their enterprises was singled out for particular condemnation. The scale of Jewish land purchases was commented upon, and the commission forecast the creation of a landless, expropriated Arab class.

The commission's allegations were investigated by an agrarian expert, Sir John Hope-Simpson. After a short aerial survey of Palestine he concluded that the country contained some 6.5 million arable dunams (approximately 1.6 million acres), one million of which were already in Jewish hands. Hope-Simpson estimated that some 30 percent of the Arab population was already landless and that the amount of land remaining in Arab hands would prove insufficient to divide among their offspring. He therefore advocated strict supervision of further Jewish immigration and land purchases and the protection of smallholders against proprietors who sold the land they tilled.

In a secret annex, which was not published, Hope-Simpson made a harsh attack on the Zionists: they were consciously trying to buy up all of Palestine, leaving the Arab masses without a living; the Jewish economy rested on precarious foundations, relying on donations from abroad; and the Jews were making communist experiments (i.e., the kibbutzim) that would probably shock the donors if they should ever discover to what use their money was put.

In 1930 there was a pronounced tendency on the part of the newly elected Labour party government to cut back and limit British commitments to the Jews. The colonial secretary, Lord Passfield (the Fabian socialist Sidney Webb), sympathized instinctively with the native Arabs against the colonizing Jews. In Palestine, Webb believed, he was dealing with a classic case of Western imperialism exploiting an indigenous population, albeit a backward one. His wife and ideological colleague, Beatrice Webb, was suspected of anti-Semitic tendencies. When Weizmann told her about the week-long slaughter in Palestine, she allegedly replied that she could not understand what all the fuss was about: "More people were killed each week in England in road accidents." [16]

In 1930 High Commissioner Chancellor played a role similar to that played by Samuel in 1922. In January 1930 he had written to London advocating that all preferential treatment of the Jews be ended and that the Arabs be granted self-government. He, too, warned that any further land sales to Jews would create a class of landless Arabs.

Hope-Simpson had also proposed the establishment of a large development fund to promote more intensive cultivation of Palestine, thus permitting more people to subsist off the same area of land. However, Britain was itself just sliding into the economic depression of the 1930s, and the Treasury vetoed any substantial expenditures overseas.

The Passfield White Paper (October 1930) modified Hope-Simpson's proposals, but it still recommended that

16. On Beatrice Webb's anti-Semitic tendencies, see Joseph Gorni, "Beatrice Webb's Views on Judaism and Zionism," *Jewish Social Studies* 40 (Spring 1978): 95–116.

Jewish immigration be stopped if it prevented Arabs from obtaining employment, or even if unemployment in the Jewish sector harmed the Arab economy. Alluding to Hope-Simpson's secret censures, the white paper stated that British policy would never be determined by the demands of the extremists in the Zionist camp. As in 1922 the white paper again promised self-government, beginning with a legislative council. (Secret discussions between the British and the Arabs to that end had in fact been in progress but were aborted by the 1929 riots.)

It was stated later (by the Peel Report in 1937) that the language used in 1930 had been insensitive. Having suffered terrible casualties in attacks that at times resembled pogroms, the Jews felt aggrieved that they, rather than the Arabs, had been placed in the dock. Instead of punishment to fit the crime, the Jews once more witnessed a British retreat. The Labour government was a minority one, however, and was subjected to severe attack by an opposition that found the Balfour Declaration a useful political instrument with which to assail its parliamentary opponents. None other than Ernest Bevin, then head of the powerful Transport Union, told Labour leaders that he would be unable to sponsor the Labour candidate in a critical by-election (in Whitechapel, a very "Jewish" district of London) unless the government issued a "pro-Zionist" statement. Prime Minister Ramsay MacDonald agreed to set up a cabinet committee, on which the Zionist leaders were invited to serve, that would "re-interpret" the Passfield White Paper.

The committee's deliberations were summarized in the form of a letter from MacDonald to Weizmann, which the prime minister read out in Parliament in February 1931. Not an official document, it nonetheless had the desired effect of negating the white paper (the Arabs called it the "black letter"). MacDonald reaffirmed the British government's obligation to the whole Jewish people, not just to the Yishuv. By implication, he thereby recognized the Jews' historic links with Palestine and the government's obligation to facilitate immigration and settlement. As a gesture to the Jews, MacDonald stated explicitly that it was not the government's intention to restrict land sales. (A survey by Sir John French, a government official, ascertained in 1931 that in fact just 570 Arab families had lost their lands.)

The Arabs of Palestine acquiesced in the British reversal of policy. In return, the administration agreed to postpone indefinitely the electoral reform of the SMC (thereby relieving the mufti of the need to stand for re-election as president of the council) and its administration of Waqf funds. However, the Arabs took note of the process whereby the supposedly objective findings of an independent commission could be reversed by the Jewish lobby in London.

The MacDonald letter was perhaps Weizmann's greatest diplomatic coup, one he would try in vain to repeat in other circumstances from 1939 on. In this instance, invaluable time was gained in which the Yishuv was strengthened immeasurably by the growing wave of immigration from anti-Semitic Europe during the early 1930s. By 1936, the year of the Arab rebellion in Palestine, the economic, industrial, and military foundations of the future Jewish state had been laid.

A critical feature of this consolidation was the sustained population increase of the Yishuv, fueled by ever-increasing immigration from Central and Eastern Europe. Jewish immigration began to surge in 1932, when 4,000 Jews arrived; it soared to 37,000 in 1933, 45,000 in 1934, and to an all-time peak of 61,000 in 1935. In addition, the British estimated that a total of 40,000 Jews had entered Palestine without legal certificates during the period from 1920 to 1939. In any event, between 1929, the year of the Wailing Wall disturbances, and 1936, that of the Arab revolt, the Jewish population of Palestine increased from 170,000 or 17 percent of the entire population, to 400,000, some 31 percent of the total. (The Arab population in 1936 was estimated at 940,000, a growth of just under 50 percent since 1918.)

The unprecedented surge in the Jewish population, apparently unhampered by the British, inevitably led the Arabs to conclude that should the current rate of Jewish immigration continue, it would not take too long before the Jews became a majority in the country. It should be recalled, too, that during this same time Jewish land purchases began to concentrate on lands owned by resident Palestinians, including land held by small owners and frequently worked by resident tenants, whereas previously the market had been largely in unoccupied or uncultivated lands owned by absentee landlords.

The Arab Rebellion

In April 1936 an Arab attack on a Jewish bus led to a series of incidents that soon escalated into nationwide disturbances. A Higher Arab Committe (HAC), a loose coalition of the recently formed political parties, was formed within a few days. It soon declared a national strike in support of three basic demands; cessation of Jewish immigration, an end to all further land sales to the Jews, and the establishment of a national (i.e., Arab) government.

These demands had in fact been under discussion with High Commissioner Wauchope since the previous summer. On Wauchope's recommendation a further proposal for a legislative council had been brought before Parliament in March, but it had been defeated in a humiliating fashion. It was perhaps this last development that convinced the Arabs that only by resorting to violence once again would they have any effect on London. The Palestinians were also encouraged by the success of a national strike by the Syrian Arabs against the French mandate and by the pressure exerted by the Egyptians on the British to renegotiate their treaty.

The deterioration in Palestine occurred at a crossroads in Britain's global strategic planning. Faced with three potential enemies—Germany, Japan, and Italy—Britain had to marshal its limited resources and fix priorities. A new five-year defense budget focused on Germany and Japan as the two countries against which British defenses would have to be prepared, and it directed that all effort be made to keep Italy at least benevolently neutral. This latter directive was of particular relevance in the Middle East, which in 1935–1936 was shocked by the way the great powers stood by, apparently helpless, as Italy overran Ethiopia with relative impunity and great brutality. When the British-inspired campaign to impose League of Nations sanctions on Italy failed, it was regarded by the Arabs as a failure not of the league but of the British.

In 1937 and 1938, after its failure to prevent the Italian conquest of Ethiopia, Britain signed two agreements with Italy affirming the status quo in the Middle East, which meant British recognition and legitimation of the Italian conquest. British planning for the Middle East in the event of war provided for the fleet to be transferred from the eastern Mediterranean to protect the empire in the Far East, leaving France to deal with Italy. Britain would leave a Middle East reserve brigade to protect its interests until the battles in the main theaters of war had been won. Unable to station an impressive military force in the Middle East, the British would have to try to hold on to the area by political appeasement and economic inducement. This policy of appeasing Italy, which had to be predicated on Arab friendship, was in gestation when the Arab rebellion erupted.

The rebellion in Palestine lasted intermittently for three years, with a "cease-fire" from October 1936 until the summer of 1937, when it flared up again after the government's endorsement of the Peel plan to partition Palestine. There was a constant feud between the army, which demanded a free hand to suppress the rebels and restore order, and the administration, which sought a political solution by acceding to some of the Arabs' demands and opposed any vigorous repression that would leave behind a sullen, embittered population. The result was vacillation, inconsistency, and a failure of government will during the early stages of the rebellion, when it might have been nipped in the bud. On the contrary, the Arabs must have been encouraged by the secret mediation of Iraq and Saudi Arabia, which all but secured a suspension of Jewish immigration as the price for a cease-fire. The secret talks were protracted, and finally aborted when Zionist intelligence leaked them to the press.

The Arab rebellion was not a military success, nor did it of itself secure the political concessions it aspired to. It did have some critical long-term consequences, however. The most important of these was the involvement of the Arab states as advocates of the Palestinian Arabs. Coming at a juncture when the British were seeking the support of the Arab world in the anticipated global conflict, this development forced Britain to regard Palestine in its Pan-Arab context, where formerly it had been able to isolate its commitments in Palestine from those in neighboring countries.

The pressure now exerted by the Arab states would cause the British cabinet first to reverse its endorsement of partition and then to invite the Arab states to a conference in 1939 to reach an agreed policy to replace the one laid down by the 1922 white paper.

The Yishuv drew several object lessons from the Arab rebellion. It was served notice once more of its vulnerability to Arab attack and boycott. The Zionists, too, attained some long-term gains; the strike of Arab dockworkers at Jaffa led to the replacement of that port by Haifa as the main entrepôt of Palestine; the Arabs' agricultural boycott forced the Jewish economy to greater self-sufficiency; and the borders indicated by the Peel partition plan, drawn usually along the lines of existing Jewish settlement, taught Yishuv economists not to determine the geographical location of future Jewish settlements according to economic criteria alone, but more in line with the areas to be claimed for the future Jewish state.

The 1939 White Paper and World War II

The white paper published by the British government in May 1939 marked the end of Britain's commitment to the Jews under the Balfour Declaration. It provided for the establishment of a Palestinian (Arab) state within ten years and the appointment of Palestinian ministers to begin taking over the government as soon as "peace and order" were restored to Palestine; a further 75,000 Jews would be allowed into Palestine over the next five years, after which all further immigration would be subject to Arab consent; all further land sales would be severely restricted.

The white paper was never endorsed by the League of Nations, and the Zionists never agreed to its terms. In 1939 Britain lost the allegiance of the Yishuv. The British

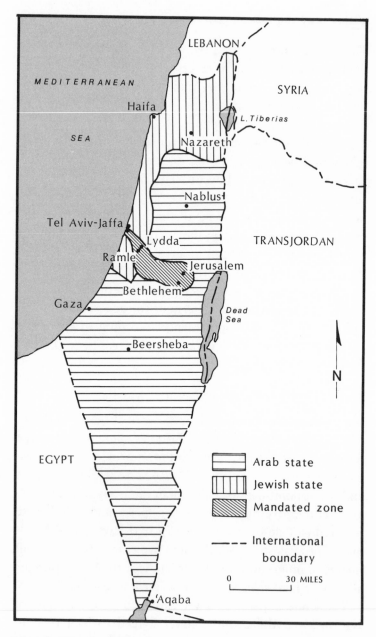

MEDITERRANEAN

Haifa

L. Tiberias

SEA

Nazareth

Nablus

Tel Aviv-Jaffa

Lydda

Ramle

Jerusalem

Bethlehem

Gaza

Dead Sea

Beersheba

LEBANON

SYRIA

TRANSJORDAN

EGYPT

N

'Aqaba

Arab state

Jewish state

Mandated zone

International boundary

0   30 MILES

Map 4. The Royal Commission (Peel) Partition Plan,
July 1937

would continue to rule Palestine as a colonial outpost, resorting yet more frequently to "emergency" regulations.

But neither did British concessions secure the sought-after agreement of the Arabs. The government had gone out of its way to gain the assent, at least, of the Arab states. At the London conference, when all negotiations with the Zionists and Palestinians had ceased, the British pressed on with the Arab states alone; again, after the conference broke up, further negotiations took place at Cairo between the British side and the Arab states. Although additional concessions were made at Cairo, the Arab states, in the face of Palestinian intransigence, dared not "betray" the Arab cause by agreeing to the British proposals. A Colonial Office official noted in retrospect:

> At an early stage in the London Conference, the British delegation (more particularly the Foreign Office representatives) were anxious to achieve by all possible means a settlement which would be accepted, if not by the Jews and the Palestinian Arabs, at least by the Arab States, and they were perhaps rather too optimistic as to the prospects of obtaining such a settlement.[17]

The leaders of the Palestinians lacked the vision to accept the future promised by the white paper. Haj Amin himself largely determined the HAC's negative response, possibly hoping that even better terms might be obtained once Britain was actually at war. Barred from returning to Palestine by the British, Haj Amin fled from Beirut to Baghdad at the outbreak of war, and from there helped engineer

17. Note by Harold F. Downie, 28 August 1940, quoted in Michael J. Cohen, *Palestine: Retreat from the Mandate, 1936–1945* (New York, 1978), pp. 86–87.

the pro-Axis Rashid Ali coup in May 1941. When the rebellion collapsed he fled to Berlin, where his active collaboration with the Nazi regime fatally compromised his own reputation and the cause of his people. In Palestine itself the Arabs in fact displayed increasing acquiescence to British rule during World War II.

After the war, there emerged something of a political stalemate between the weakened clans on the one hand, many of whose leaders were either exiled or discredited, and the new urban elites on the other hand. The Husaynis' grip on Palestine was weakened by the increasing gap between their social sources of power and the new realities of economic and social life. The Palestinians' difficulties and their inability to organize themselves led to the ever-increasing involvement of the Arab League in internal Palestinian Arab politics. The mufti himself remained excluded from Palestine by the British. But from his exile in Cairo he continued to influence events in Palestine and prevented the growth of any political alternatives. He secured the sponsorship of the Egyptians, who used him as a foil against ʿAbdallah's interest in annexing Palestine. In turn, ʿAbdallah sponsored the Nashashibi position. Thus traditional rivalries were seized upon and perpetuated by inter-Arab contests.

There can be no doubt that the 1939 white paper brought about a radicalization of the Yishuv and ultimately provoked it into open rebellion after the war. Britain was severely limiting the Zionists' options just at the time of their greatest need. It must be emphasized, however, that the new course in Zionist policy was determined before the first details of the Holocaust were received, let alone believed. The final break with Great Britain came not with the white paper but at the end of 1941, when the Churchill government rejected the Zionists' proposals to set up a Jewish division within the British army.

Inevitably, Britain's gallant fight against Nazism had been regarded by the Jews as their cause too, even if the Chamberlain government had cold-shouldered the Zionist offers of military aid. The advent of the Churchill government in May 1940, however, seemed to presage a change of political fortune for the Zionists. Even David Ben-Gurion, who scarcely three months before had advocated open rebellion against Britain for promulgating the white paper land regulations, now granted Churchill a period of grace to allow him to reverse the policy he had so castigated in opposition.

Churchill's innate sympathy for the Zionists seemed at first to augur well. He believed that the raising of a Jewish force in Palestine would enable him to bring back to England the eleven British battalions tied down in Palestine. Moreover, mindful of the precedent of World War I, Churchill was very much preoccupied with mobilizing Jewish aid in America to bring the United States into the war.

However, the successful pursuit of the war was for Churchill his all-excluding priority. When his chiefs of staff stood firm against the return of British troops from the Middle East (because it would take too long and would cause a fatal decline in British prestige throughout the Middle East), Churchill gave in. Although the cabinet agreed in September 1940 to the formation of a Jewish division, the proposal was stifled by departmental officials and military experts. They all warned of Arab rebellion in protest against the British helping the Jews take over Palestine by force. Churchill expended much rhetoric against the military's objections (and against General Wavell personally), but he did not overrule them. The project was eventually shelved indefinitely in October 1941, with apparently little intervention by Churchill himself.

The Zionist leadership had split over the Jewish Division scheme. Weizmann had looked primarily to the diplomatic rewards to be reaped in return for Jewish participation in the Allied war effort. In contrast, Ben-Gurion was concerned primarily with self-defense in Palestine and insisted that the Jewish division serve only in Palestine. Even when the issue was rendered academic in October 1941, Ben-Gurion seized on Weizmann's handling of the negotiations as a pretext for challenging the latter's leadership.

The cancellation of the Jewish Division scheme also marked Ben-Gurion's final disillusion with Great Britain and the transfer of his attentions to the United States. With nothing more to be gained from the traditional alliance with Britain, he believed also that the time had come to demand in public the establishment of a Jewish state as part of the new world order after the war. This concept found its expression in the so-called Biltmore Programme, decided upon by an extraordinary meeting of the American Zionists (attended by both Ben-Gurion and Weizmann) in May 1942. As we have already noted, the new policy was adopted *before* the extent of the Nazi killings in Europe was known.

Weizmann had in fact preceded the Biltmore Programme with his own call for a Jewish commonwealth in an article published in *Foreign Affairs* in January 1942. But Weizmann and Ben-Gurion differed radically in their interpretations of the new Zionist policy. Weizmann, who was emotionally and intellectually incapable of making a complete break with Britain, saw the new policy simply as a basis for negotiations, from which a tactical retreat to partition might be made. In contrast, Ben-Gurion envisaged solving the Yishuv's demographic problems (i.e., its minority status) by a one-time migration of two to three million Jews within a year or two of the end of the war. Tragically, Ben-Gurion's messianic vision did not foresee that there would be no millions of Jews after the war who could turn the vision into reality.

The failure of the Jewish division scheme and Ben-Gurion's success in converting the Zionist movement to his interpretation of the Biltmore Programme marked the end of Weizmann's ascendancy. The British took note of the schism and the emergence of Ben-Gurion's "extremist" school. In an effort to strengthen the "moderate" camp, the British belatedly agreed in September 1944 to the formation of a Jewish brigade, provided it did not serve in the Middle East. The new unit was one-third the size of the division originally asked for and was not even allowed to wear its Jewish insignia while in transit through Egypt. At the same time, the British dropped frequent hints that a new partition scheme was under consideration by the cabinet and that after the war the Jews would be allotted the biggest "plum" in the Middle East "pudding."

The perceived need for Britain to appease the Arabs did not pass with the British victories after El Alamein. To the contrary, the war brought an increased appreciation of Middle East oil reserves and heightened British fears about Soviet and American activity in the Middle East. The Foreign Office now warned that should Britain make a wrong move in Palestine (i.e., by a retreat from the 1939 white paper), either of Britain's current allies would be only too pleased to take over the hegemony Britain had enjoyed between the wars. Foreign Office warnings took on more substance when, in March 1945, the Arab states united in the Arab League.

The British did not in fact initiate the establishment of the Arab League, although Anthony Eden's famous Mansion House speech at the end of May 1941 undoubtedly encouraged the Arabs. Eden's speech proffered British support for any Arab initiative on the eve of the British invasion of Vichy Syria. It was a piece of pure propaganda, designed to persuade the Arabs that Britain would support their aspirations to independence and unity. But when the Arabs then asked the government what Eden's speech had meant, Whitehall instigated an analysis of the prospects for Arab unity from the point of view of British interests. The official report concluded with a warning that the Arab desire for unity in fact reflected a wish to form a bloc strong enough to resist Western imperialism in the Middle East—the British in Egypt and Palestine (where Britain propped up the Zionist cause) and the French in Syria. However, when in 1944 the Arabs, against all British prognostications, took the first steps in setting up their league, the Middle East ambassadors were quick to perceive the new challenges and opportunity represented by the new body.[18]

When the representatives of the Arab states first convened at Alexandria from September to October 1944, the joint protocol they signed at long last recognized the 1939 white paper as establishing the rights of the Palestinian Arabs. Whereas the British had tried in vain to secure Arab support for their Palestinian policy in 1939, in 1944 that support was retroactively given without British solicitation. The Foreign Office could now argue with more con-

18. On the foundation of the Arab League, see Cohen, *Palestine: Retreat from the Mandate,* chap. 8; and Ahmad M. Gomaa, *The Foundation of the League of Arab States: Wartime Diplomacy and Inter-Arab Politics, 1941–1945* (London, 1978).

viction that any retreat from the white paper would incur for Britain the wrath of a united Arab world.

In November 1944, less than a month after the signing of the Alexander protocol, another event of critical significance occurred. Lord Moyne, the British minister-resident in Cairo, was assassinated by Jewish terrorists. This act, in fact carried out by the smaller and less significant of the two Jewish terrorist groups, the Lehi, brought to a climax a series of attacks on the British. The terrorist campaign waged by Menahem Begin's Irgun had begun at the start of 1944, fueled by sentiments of frustration and desperation over the white paper, which from March 1944 threatened to close Palestine to all further immigration.

The mainstream members of the Yishuv were caught in a terrible dilemma. On the one hand, if they allowed terrorism to run amok in their community, it might destroy the moral and political fabric of the new society they were trying to build. In addition, some leaders, such as Ben-Gurion himself, feared that the dissidents aimed at nothing less than a fascist coup to unseat the workers' political hegemony. But on the other hand, the terrorists were at least *doing* something, registering a protest against the white paper policy in Palestine. Moreover, and perhaps above all, how could Jews in Palestine cooperate with the British regime against members of their own community, when the British were behaving in such a callous fashion toward the Jews in Europe?

During the summer months of 1944 Jewish opinion across the globe was particularly incensed by the Allies' apparent indifference to the plight of the European Jews. Two separate plans to bring some relief had, after much procrastination, been turned down by the Allies. The first was a plan to save the remnants of Hungary's 800,000 Jews in return for a ransom of 10,000 trucks and other nonmilitary supplies to the Germans. The offer, from Adolf Eichmann himself, was brought to the West by Joel Brand, a Zionist official from Budapest. It was soon discovered that Brand's companion, Bundy Grosz, was a double agent, acting on behalf of the S.S. chief, Himmler, who was seeking a separate peace with the West. Himmler promised that the matériel requested would not be employed against the West but would be reserved for use on the Eastern Front against the Russians. The plan was rejected by the West on the grounds that there could be no negotiations with the Germans short of an absolute and unconditional surrender. Even if it did occur to anyone at the time that the mere process of negotiation might have held up the deportations to Auschwitz, thereby saving countless lives, this tactic was not in fact considered seriously.

The second plan, submitted to the British government by the Jewish Agency in July 1944, was to bomb the Auschwitz death camp and/or the railway lines leading to it, an operation that might have sabotaged the Nazi death machine, even if only for a time. In addition, it would have made it clear to the Nazi regime, as no other message could, that the West regarded their behavior toward the Jews as beyond standards acceptable to Western civilization. By July 1944, as the Zionists informed Eden and Churchill, one and a half million Jews had already been put to death in Auschwitz alone. But once again, the Jews were told that the Allies' military priorities precluded any special action on their behalf and that they would have to wait, along with other oppressed peoples, for the ultimate liberation of Europe. The Jews were told that the Allied air forces did not have the range to reach the camp, when at the very time Allied planes were in fact practically overflying Auschwitz. (The I. G. Farben plants in the Auschwitz industrial area, less than five miles from the death camp, and the huge oil-refining complex at Blechhammer, just forty-seven miles from Auschwitz, were major strategic targets; in addition, the fleets of Allied aircraft that dropped supplies to the doomed revolt of the Polish Home Army during the month of August 1944 also flew virtually over the Auschwitz death camp.) The Auschwitz camp was indeed photographed and bombed by Allied planes—by mistake![19] Britain's failure to respond even tactically to the Brand mission, and its continued adherence to the immigration restrictions, did nothing to endear the British to the Yishuv in Palestine.

There was also a direct connection between the Brand mission and the Moyne assassination. The Lehi explained later that they had chosen Moyne as their victim not only because of his earlier anti-Zionist record as colonial secretary (he was blamed for the sinking of the ship *Struma* in February 1942, with the loss of all but one of its complement of illegal immigrants), but also because when he had interviewed Brand in Cairo, he had allegedly rebuffed Brand by asking rhetorically, "But where will we put all those [Hungarian] Jews?"

The Zionist leadership, too, had its priorities. With the

19. On the Brand mission, and the plans to bomb Auschwitz, see Bernard Wasserstein, *Britain and the Jews of Europe, 1939–1945* (Oxford, 1979), pp. 249–263, 307–320; and Michael J. Cohen, *Churchill and the Jews* (London, 1985), pp. 286–305. On the projected Auschwitz operation, see, especially, Martin Gilbert, *Auschwitz and the Allies* (New York, 1981); and David Wyman, "Why Auschwitz Was Never Bombed," *Commentary* 65 (May 1978): 37–46. For a recent condemnation of Allied, especially American, inaction, see David Wyman, *The Abandonment of the Jews* (New York, 1984).

assassination of Moyne, it seemed to them that a terrorist minority was jeopardizing the whole community's political future. The Jewish Brigade had just been formed, and British statesmen, including Churchill, had dropped frequent hints that after the war the Zionists would receive a "generous" partition in which to build up their own state in Palestine. Following the Moyne murder, Churchill himself (Moyne had been his personal friend) issued the following unprecedentedly harsh public warning to the Zionists in the House of Commons:

> If our dreams for Zionism are to end in the smoke of assassins' pistols and our labours for its future to produce only a new set of gangsters worthy of Nazi Germany, many like myself will have to consider the position we have maintained so consistently in the past.[20]

So in November 1944 the Jewish Agency's clandestine military arm, the Hagana, moved against the Irgun, either incarcerating its members in patched-up prisons of their own or turning them over to the British. The Lehi, whose men had in fact murdered Moyne, had agreed to cease all further terrorism and was not harmed. This operation, known as the *saison* (literally, hunting season), was one of the bitterest in the Yishuv's history, as personal and political scores became at times intermingled with concern for the national destiny.

But it was all apparently in vain. The Churchill government shelved the partition plan that had been ready for cabinet consideration, and no British government ever again

20. Churchill, Speech to the House of Commons, 17 November 1944, *Parliamentary Debates* (Commons), 5th ser., vol. 404, col. 2242, quoted in Cohen, *Churchill and the Jews,* p. 258.

considered the possibility of setting up a Jewish state in Palestine. Churchill himself made no further contribution to the Zionist struggle for independence. In July 1945, barely weeks before his own defeat at the polls, he made the following response to mounting American criticism of Britain's refusal to allow more Jews into Palestine:

> I do not think that we should take the responsibility upon ourselves of managing this very difficult place while the Americans sit back and criticise. . . . I am not aware of the slightest advantage which has ever accrued to Great Britain from this painful and thankless task. Somebody else should have their turn now.[21]

21. Churchill to Colonial Office and chiefs of staff, 6 July 1945, E4939, FO 371/45378.

CHAPTER FOUR

From Mandate
to Independence,
1945–1948

The Power Vacuum in 1945

By 1945 the complex interests clashing in Palestine had rendered that country's problems intractable and the mandatory regime unmanageable. The determination of both Jews and Arabs to fight for what each considered inviolable rights ruled out all prospects of compromise. As Palestine was included in the Labour government's decolonization trend and the British lost the will to impose a solution on the two sides, war in Palestine became inevitable.

Britain's decision to relinquish the mandate was determined largely by its inability to arrive at a consensus with the United States. Yet even without President Harry Truman's frequent interventions, it seems doubtful whether Britain could have stayed on in Palestine—except in the most unlikely event that the United States were to have dispatched troops to Palestine to help the British maintain order. It is apposite to remember that in February 1947, the month in which they referred the Palestine mandate to the United Nations, the British also decided to evacuate India and informed the Americans that Britain could no longer carry the military burdens of shoring up Greece and Turkey against communist encroachment. (This last communication, made in a private letter from Foreign Minister Ernest Bevin, led to the Truman Doctrine, announced by the president before the U.S. Congress a month later.)

The period between the end of World War II and the establishment of the state of Israel in 1948 was one of great turmoil in Palestine itself and of intense diplomatic activity in Western capitals. Tension was kept high by the survivors of the Nazi death camps, who crowded in ever-increasing numbers into the displaced persons (DP) camps in those parts of Germany and Austria occupied by the Allies.

The inability of Britain and the United States to reach a consensus on Palestine left greater room for maneuver by the local minor powers. The impotence of the Palestinian Arabs and the chronic disunity within the Arab League in turn permitted the Jews and King ʿAbdallah to gain the maximum advantage from the power vacuum that followed Britain's decision to evacuate. Indeed, the Jews and ʿAbdallah, commanding the two most effective military forces in the area, tried repeatedly, in vain, to negotiate the partition of Palestine.

The Search for an Anglo-American Consensus

The Labour government's consideration of long-term policy in Palestine was cut short by rising American pressures to allow 100,000 Jewish DPs immediate entry into Palestine. (The British held the immigration quota to 1,500 per month.) In an attempt to involve the United States in the search for a solution to the problem, Bevin initiated the appointment of a joint Anglo-American committee of inquiry to consider possible havens for the refugees, including, at American insistence, Palestine itself.

Bevin relied on the Americans to hold off Soviet encroachments in the Near East and Iran. He warned that American support for the Zionist cause in Palestine would alienate the Arab world from the West, thereby bringing about the same development they were both determined to avert along the Northern tier (Greece, Turkey, and Iran)— Soviet encroachment. In addition, good relations between Britain and the United States, which might be wrecked over the emotions generated by the Palestine issue, were a prerequisite for congressional approval of the huge American loan to Britain, negotiated in Washington during the fall of 1945 and debated in Congress the following year.

Attempts to analyze the significance of the joint Anglo-American committee have given rise to several historical distortions. When Bevin met with the committee members in London, he apparently promised them that if their report was unanimous, it would be implemented. This commitment greatly influenced the committee's final deliberations, persuading those who had opted for partition to give up their proposal, in return for which they expected Bevin to implement their recommendation to allow the 100,000 DPs into Palestine. Within months of returning from Palestine in 1946, two of the pro-Zionists on the committee, Richard Crossman from England and Bartley Crum from the United States, both of whom had favored partition, published books indicting Bevin. They both accused Bevin of breaking his promise to implement the joint committee's report.[1]

The Zionists' and Truman's policy laid great emphasis on the proposal to dispatch the 100,000 DPs to Palestine, as have subsequent "historical" accounts. This single aspect

---

1. Richard H. Crossman, *Palestine Mission* (London, 1947); and Bartley Crum, *Behind the Silken Curtain* (New York, 1947).

has been stressed to the exclusion of all others, and it has frequently been suggested that had the British only agreed to Truman's demand, Zionist ambitions might have been nipped in the bud—their campaign for a Jewish state would have been headed off and Truman might have ceased to intervene on the Jews' behalf.

When the Anglo-American committee's report was delivered to London and Washington in April 1946, it was again this proposal concerning the displaced persons that was highlighted exclusively. Under Zionist pressure Truman announced his support for their immigration without so much as consulting the British first. But the Zionists' support for this proposal (the first of many in the report) was purely tactical. The Zionists would have rejected the report had they been asked to accept it in toto or not at all. Ben-Gurion thought that the report presaged a return to the 1939 white paper regime. Although the 100,000 might be allowed in, future immigration policy would be left to the trustee's (i.e., Britain's) discretion. Likewise, although the 1940 land regulations were to be rescinded, the future economic development of Palestine was to be predicated on "ensuring the rights and conditions of other sections of the population." But the British did not intend to be pushed into implementing the particular part of the report Truman and the Zionists liked, while rejecting the rest. Among its other proposals, for example, the report recommended that Palestine never become either a Jewish or an Arab state.

In retrospect it may be asked whether the British would really have solved the whole problem by allowing an additional 100,000 Jews into Palestine and leaving it at that. Given that the Palestinian Arabs had rebelled in 1936 largely because of Jewish immigration in the early 1930s, could a further rebellion, this time backed by the Arab

League, have been ruled out if Britain went so much over the limits already promised to the Arabs in the 1939 white paper? Furthermore, could the Zionists themselves have settled for a limit of 100,000, when by the summer of 1946 the ranks of Jewish displaced persons had swelled to over 250,000, their number augmented by Jews in flight from pogroms in Poland? Would the Jews then have abandoned the Biltmore Programme and all other hopes of sovereignty?

The joint committee had also warned explicitly against permitting any of the illegal private armies in Palestine to sabotage the solution it proposed. When Truman seized upon a single recommendation, the immigration of the 100,000, the British responded by demanding the disbanding of the "secret armies" prior to any increase in immigration. From the British point of view, the elementary requirements of security dictated this step. Indeed, anticipating Arab disorders in the event of such large-scale Jewish immigration, Bevin asked how many American troops the United States was willing to commit to preserve law and order in Palestine. From the Jewish point of view, however, it was absurd even to contemplate any voluntary surrender of their only means of self-defense, be it against the Arabs or even against the British themselves. The Jews concluded that London was willfully sabotaging the committee's report and had no intention of allowing in the 100,000.

The records indicate that the British had every intention of allowing in the 100,000, however, provided this was done within the framework of a comprehensive political settlement, and provided the Americans furnished the necessary political, economic, and military aid to implement such a settlement. To that end, talks were held between British and American experts in London in July 1946.

The so-called experts talks led to a new scheme, the Morrison-Grady plan for "provincial autonomy" in Palestine. The plan also provided for the migration of the 100,000—indeed, the talks had been preceded by Anglo-American talks in London to figure out the logistics of transferring such large numbers. Provincial autonomy, a British scheme devised during the war, was a compromise designed to give each community some outlet for its national aspirations, while reserving British federal control.

The plan also had several tactical attractions. First, since it did not involve any significant change in the mandatory regime, provincial autonomy would not need to be referred to the United Nations, where foreign elements might interfere with British interests. Second, the plan might be dressed up to fit in with the aspirations of both Arabs and Jews: the Arabs could be led to hope that the two provinces might be united ultimately into a single, Palestinian state; and the Zionists could be led to hope exactly the opposite—that separation would be permanent, with each province developing into a sovereign state.

But neither Jews nor Arabs retained sufficient trust in the British to waive immediate sovereignty. Once again, Zionist pressure ensured that Truman did not endorse the Morrison-Grady plan, although he did not reject it either, as has often been inferred. On 5 September 1946 Truman told a press conference that the plan was still under consideration and that the administration was contemplating a $300 million loan to finance it. Furthermore, in his so-called Yom Kippur speech of 4 October, Truman in fact expressed his desire to see a compromise solution evolve between the British plan and that of the Jewish Agency (partition). The Zionists were particularly enraged by the British condition that the immigration of the 100,000, which they believed they had already secured the previous April, was now mortgaged to the complete implementation of the provincial autonomy plan. With their opposition to provincial autonomy, they were in effect made to defer the 100,000 also.

Truman was by now so frustrated and embittered that he refused to receive anyone from the Jewish lobby in the White House. He blamed the Zionists for having sabotaged what he saw as a viable solution. It was the threat that Truman might in fact withdraw completely that forced the Zionists to a sober reappraisal of their policy during the summer of 1946. This turn of events was dictated by the evident failure of the radically militant policy adopted by the Zionists the previous autumn.

Zionist Rebellion

The Zionist leadership had been thoroughly disillusioned with the British Labour government when it failed to carry out its election platform regarding Palestine. During the election campaign, the Labour party not only had promised to support the establishment of a Jewish state in Palestine but also, to the considerable embarrassment of most Zionists, had proposed the transfer of Palestine's Arabs to neighboring Arab states. Bevin's blunt manner soon put off the Zionists, who concluded that he had fallen completely under the influence of his pro-Arab advisers at the Foreign Office.

The Zionists concluded prematurely that the Labour government intended to implement the 1939 white paper to its constitutional end—that is, until the establishment of a Palestinian state. Under Ben-Gurion's direction, the Jewish Agency decided in October of 1945 to unite with the

Jewish dissident groups in a combined rebellion against the British administration in Palestine. Ben-Gurion believed that he could strengthen his diplomatic bargaining hand by posing strategic threats to the British in Palestine, rendering the country useless as a military base. Thus the two major operations carried out by the Hagana—inflicting extensive sabotage to Palestine's railway system on the night of 31 October 1945, and destroying all but one of Palestine's bridges to neighboring countries on 17 June 1946—both paralyzed communications and caused the British grave logistical problems.

In contrast, Begin's Irgun rejected diplomacy out of hand and counted on armed revolt to drive the British out of Palestine. The Irgun attacked British army camps, destroyed army stores and airplanes, ambushed army vehicles, and in general tried to destroy the British will to rule in Palestine. The Irgun's more extremist offshoot, the Lehi, concentrated on personal terror. So each organization pursued its own goals and strategy—the Irgun tried to erode the morale of the British army, the Lehi tried to make Palestine a place unsafe for British personnel, and the Hagana for the most part concentrated on immobilizing the patrol boats and radar stations that were apprehending most of those Jewish immigrants trying to enter Palestine without official permits.

The rebellion was a failure, at least from the Jewish Agency's point of view. Ben-Gurion had given the word to start the rebellion without knowing that at that moment negotiations were afoot to bring the Americans into the picture. Had he known, it seems doubtful that he would have taken the same step. Neither did the Hagana seriously impair British ability to detect and detain illegal immigrants.

On the contrary, the British countermeasures in reaction to the Hagana operation of 17 June 1946 only served to severely undermine the Yishuv's confidence in its own leaders.

On Saturday, 29 June 1946, some 17,000 British troops rounded up nearly 3,000 Jews, including most of the Jewish Agency leadership and the Hagana's officer cadre. Many felt that their leaders' militancy had brought them to the brink of war with the British regime—a premature war with the wrong party. The Hagana in fact never operated against the British again, and the Jewish Agency moderated its diplomatic line.

The Jewish Agency broke finally with the Irgun and Lehi after the Irgun's attack on the King David Hotel in Jerusalem on 24 July 1946. The Hagana had in fact helped to plan that attack and had tried to influence the detailed planning of the operation. The King David Hotel was used as headquarters by the top civil and military personnel of the British administration, and many top Arab and Jewish civil servants worked there, too. There is some confusion and disagreement over whether the Irgun's telephone warnings arrived in time to permit the evacuation of the hotel. It is a fact, however, that nearly a hundred British, Arab, and Jewish officials lost their lives in the explosion. The Yishuv was saved this time from British reprisals by London's concern that nothing be done to upset the recently agreed-upon Morrison-Grady plan (Truman had yet to back down).

The Jewish Agency, sharing the Yishuv's shock at the unanticipated magnitude of the disaster, took the opportunity to disassociate itself from the Irgun, which for obscure reasons concurred in the agency's demand that it, the Irgun, take sole public responsibility for the attack. Ben-Gurion, the advocate of militancy, now conceded the political limelight to a relative newcomer, the moderate Nahum Goldmann.

A special session of the Jewish Agency executive, convened in Paris in August 1946 to discuss whether to continue the rebellion, found its discussions dominated by Truman's threat to withdraw his support unless the Zionists themselves came up with a reasonably acceptable political plan. Many of those who had opposed the Peel partition plan in 1937 now professed their regret at their shortsightedness—had the Jews had their own state during the war, they would have been able to do more for the deserted Jews in Europe. Similarly, while the Zionists had stuck resolutely to their political guns, the Jewish DPs, now numbering over a quarter of a million, were facing the prospect of a second European winter in makeshift camps. In a general climate of remorse and frustration, the agency executive decided by a majority to abandon the Biltmore Programme and to settle for a viable state in a part of Palestine—that is, for partition.

Goldmann, one of the agency representatives in the United States, was dispatched in mid-session to fly to Washington on a mission to secure the president's and the administration's support for the "new" Zionist policy. On his return Goldmann tried to convince his colleagues in Paris and the British that Truman would support partition. The Americans declined to assume an active role, though, hoping that the Zionists and the British would arrive at some compromise between provincial autonomy and partition. The omens seemed good—the Yishuv was in a subdued mood, and the moderate Goldmann had been allowed to take over Zionist diplomacy.

Goldmann himself was largely responsible for the illusions entertained by Washington and London, however. In his talks with Under Secretary of State Dean Acheson in Washington and with Bevin in Paris, Goldmann had conveyed the false impression that the Zionists would settle for provincial autonomy as a first step to partition. Bevin was convinced that he was at last on the brink of the long-sought breakthrough.

At this delicate stage of the proceedings, Truman once more intervened on 4 October, Yom Kippur eve. With congressional elections pending, Truman was constrained once more to make a public play for the Jewish vote. Truman's "Yom Kippur" speech has also been subject to numerous misinterpretations. It was generally misconstrued at the time (and has been since) as an expression of presidential support for the Zionist program, partition.[2] The impression left by the speech was perhaps more important than what Truman in fact said. However, Truman did speak specifically of a compromise being reached between the Zionist and British plans. Significantly, as was noted ruefully by some

2. For example, Robert J. Donovan, in his biography of Truman (*Conflict and Crisis: The Presidency of Harry S. Truman, 1945–1948* [New York, 1977]), quotes the part of Truman's speech referring to the administration's willingness to support the Jewish Agency scheme, and continues, "Thus for the first time [Truman] publicly lent his backing to the creation of a 'viable' Jewish State in Palestine" (p. 321). However, further on in the speech, which had referred to both British and Zionist plans, the president concluded: "I cannot believe that the gap between the proposals which have been put forward is too great to be bridged by men of reason and goodwill." For the text of the speech, see *Foreign Relations of the United States,* vol. 7: *1946* (Washington, D.C., 1971), p. 703. The Zionists submitted the original draft of the Yom Kippur statement to the White House, which referred it to the State Department, where the "bridging the gap" amendment was added. See Eliahu Elath, *Struggle for Statehood,* vol. 1: *1945–1948* (Tel Aviv, 1979), pp. 424–425 (in Hebrew).

Zionist observers at the time, Truman also dropped the "100,000" formula, stating his desire to see "substantial immigration," a somewhat vague conception.

Truman's "Yom Kippur" speech marked a political watershed. Convinced that Goldmann and the Zionist moderates had been about to settle for provincial autonomy, Bevin believed that Truman's intervention had effectively spoiled any chance there might have been to reach a compromise. Truman's speech had signaled to the Zionists that the president could always be relied on to support their cause. When Bevin visited the United States in November 1946, he warned the Americans and the Zionists that if no compromise agreement could be reached, the British would pull out of Palestine. His interlocutors were alarmed, none more so than the militant Zionist leader Rabbi Abba Hillel Silver, who had criticized Bevin's policy harshly. Truman reassured Bevin in person that with no further domestic elections in prospect for some time, he would be able to afford the British greater freedom of maneuver in the pending roundtable conference on Palestine, due to be convened in London in January 1947.

Arab Disarray

As noted in chapter 3, the mandatory regime in Palestine had brought substantial socioeconomic changes to traditional Arab society. In the process, a community that had been relatively stable for generations suffered great social fragmentation. An unprecedented population explosion in the Arab community was surpassed by an even greater percentage growth of the Jewish community, owing to immigration; an influx of foreign capital, both British and Jewish, undermined the monopolistic control of the Arab landed elites. But the new prosperity had brought only greater communal strife, not political integration. With their leaders either in exile or engaged in factional struggle, the Palestinians were left without any effective leadership, and from 1944 on they became the de facto wards of the Arab League.

The Palestinians themselves viewed the Arab League's patronage with some suspicion, appreciating that each of the Arab states entertained its own particular ambitions in Palestine, which often as not also proved a useful distraction from its own domestic problems. In return, the Palestinians were later accused of not paying sufficient heed to advice given them at the time by the league, whose members were more experienced in international affairs and tended to greater flexibility and a realistic approach. The Palestinians were blamed for refusing to appear before international commissions and in other forums where they might have taken the valuable opportunity to air their case in front of those Western governments with whom their fate ultimately lay.

A new HAC was reconstituted at the end of 1945, but being dominated by the Husaynis it soon ran into a boycott by all the other parties. With the repatriation of Jemal Husayni from Rhodesia, the HAC belatedly decided to give evidence before the Anglo-American committee of inquiry, but failed to make much of an impression. At this point, the Arab League intervened, trying to bring an end to internal faction fighting and to evolve a coherent Arab policy that might be pressed on the West.

At secret meetings in May and June 1946, the Arab League convened to consider the Anglo-American committee's report. The league warned England and the United States that they risked forfeiting the friendship of the Arab world if the Palestinians' rights were prejudiced. Protest notes were sent to Western capitals, but the league's "operational" measures were kept secret. These secret options— military intervention in Palestine and economic sanctions (i.e., termination of oil concessions)—were leaked from several sources to the West. However, the Arab states were most careful to heed British warnings not to intervene in Palestine until they, the British, had left. As for an oil embargo, at that period in their history the oil-producing states in the Middle East needed hard currency more than the West needed Arab oil, and the threat to withhold Arab oil took a further twenty-five years to materialize.[3]

The Arab League was itself riven by the clashing interests of its members. Most member states were engaged in a struggle to detach themselves from the tutelage of either Britain or France, and each was concerned to display the vigor of its patriotic struggle. If certain states could not display to their people the impressive concessions from their colonial master that they had hoped for, it was relatively easy to whip up patriotic fervor over the Palestinians' cause. This was the case with both Iraq and Egypt in negotiations with Britain, and with Syria, which, negotiating with France, depended heavily on the British to rid it of French rule. ʿAbdallah, the ruler of a barren kingdom adjacent to Palestine, who since the 1930s had planned to annex the Arab West Bank to Transjordan, was a special case. This would be but the first stage in realizing his ambition to carve out for himself the greater Syrian kingdom that he believed should have been his brother's. In addition, there was Ibn Saʿūd, universally the most respected leader of the Arab world though militarily a lightweight and very much dependent on American dollars to keep his fragile desert kingdom

3. On the oil factor as an element in the Arab-Zionist conflict, see Aaron David Miller, *Search for Security: Saudi Arabian Oil and American Foreign Policy, 1939–1949* (Chapel Hill, N.C., 1980).

together. Ibn Saʿūd was most anxious lest his traditional rivals, the Hashemites, rulers of Transjordan and Iraq, should make territorial gains in Palestine and perhaps obtain a bridgehead from which to avenge the defeat of their house by Ibn Saʿūd in the 1920s.

When the United Nations unexpectedly recommended the partition of Palestine into Jewish and Arab states in November 1947, ʿAbdallah's Arab Legion was the only Arab military force ready and able to move in to aid the Palestinians. ʿAbdallah met with Zionist leaders, and each side expressed the hope that they would be able to partition Palestine between themselves in an orderly fashion. But it was the very prospect of ʿAbdallah monopolizing the territorial spoils in Palestine and the possible abandonment of western Palestine to the Jews that spurred the other Arab states to intervene. In May 1948, at a meeting with Golda Myerson (Meir), ʿAbdallah warned that the vigilance and jealousies of the other Arab states no longer permitted him to stop his invasion at the UN partition lines. Unwilling to permit such a radical, unilateral alteration of the status quo in the Arab world, four other Arab armies joined ʿAbdallah's forces in a joint, if not coordinated, invasion of Israel on the first day of its independence, 15 May 1948.

The British Decision to Surrender the Mandate

In February 1947, when Bevin failed to secure the agreement of either the Jews or the Arabs to his final plan for graduated independence for Palestine within five years (during which there would be a further immigration of 98,000 Jews), the British cabinet decided to refer the problem to the United Nations.

Most historians have interpreted this move as a cynical ploy on Britain's part to demonstrate to the international community just how intractable the problem was; having once burned its fingers, the international community would then gladly return Palestine to Britain on the latter's terms. This conspiracy theory received support from Colonial Secretary Arthur Creech-Jones's assertion at the time that Britain was going to the United Nations only to seek advice.[4]

Like many conspiracy theories, however, this one rests on circumstantial threads of evidence. The British records make it clear beyond doubt that Bevin, the dominant figure in the British cabinet, was from the end of 1946 on not prepared to impose any solution in Palestine against Arab will. Under certain circumstances he might have trusted Truman to allow him to impose a solution unfavorable to the Jews. But the Arabs' rejection of Bevin's last proposals in February 1947 saved him from that option. Moreover, had the British really been so determined to stay on in Palestine, would they have risked foreign intervention at the United Nations? Once the United Nations came in, could Britain be certain of receiving back a mandate, or trusteeship, on acceptable terms?

Historians have been misled, too, by the evident enthusiasm for Palestine displayed by the British military, in 1946–1947 desperately searching for an alternative base to the Canal Zone in Egypt. The military, however, concentrated on their logistical problems and were slow to see the political

4. For different views on British motives for referring the Palestine question to the United Nations, compare Jacob C. Hurewitz, *The Struggle for Palestine* (New York, 1950); Michael J. Cohen, *Palestine and the Great Powers, 1945–1948* (Princeton, N.J., 1982); Ilan Amitzur, "Withdrawal Without Recommendations: Britain's Decision to Relinquish the Palestine Mandate, 1947," in *Zionism and Arabism in Palestine and Israel,* ed. Elie Kedourie and Sylvia G. Haim (London, 1982); and Michael J. Cohen's review of the Kedourie and Haim volume, *Middle Eastern Studies* 19 (July 1983): 386–392.

risks involved in holding on to a base in an area of rampant rival nationalisms. The military also agreed that any advantages to be gained by military alliances with the successor states in the event of partition would be outweighed by the adverse reactions to Britain around the Arab world. Finally, by the time the UN General Assembly came to debate the Special Committee on Palestine (UNSCOP) partition plan in autumn 1947, the Security Council had rebuffed Egypt's appeal against the retention of British bases along the canal, and thus the military's search for an alternative was allayed for the foreseeable future.

Once the problem had been referred to the United Nations, the deteriorating security situation in Palestine during the course of 1947 made it almost inconceivable that Britain could continue to hold on by itself. By 1947 Palestine was the major trouble spot in the British empire, requiring some 100,000 troops and a huge budget to maintain. Churchill poured scorn on a government that thought nothing of relinquishing imperial hold of huge territories in India and Burma yet insisted on hanging on to "tiny Palestine."

In effect, the Palestine administration's retreat before terrorism began *before* Bevin referred the problem to the United Nations. In January 1947 two British civilians were kidnapped by the Irgun—one, a judge, was abducted literally while sitting in judgment on the bench. Fearing an escalation of this type of activity, against which they had no remedy, the British evacuated some 2,000 nonessential personnel, women, and children. All remaining officials were rehoused in barbed-wire-enclosed compounds, nicknamed "Bevingrads" by the Jews.

The evacuation, during the month of February, was followed by the imposition of martial law on Tel Aviv and parts of Jerusalem on 2 March. But in the absence of any support from the Yishuv, few terrorists were caught in the British net. The Jews were in fact becoming increasingly alienated from the British regime, their emotions strained each time the British deported another transport of would-be immigrants.[5] In order to stamp out terrorism in Palestine, either the British would have required the support of a major section of the Jewish community or they would have had to employ draconian methods, inconsistent with the liberal values they preached at home, against a highly articulate community that could and did plead its cause ably in the international community.

From November 1944 until May 1945 the Yishuv had briefly cooperated with the British in their struggle to suppress Jewish terrorism. However, the campaign had been nurtured on Zionist hopes that the Churchill government would help the Jews establish a viable Jewish state in Palestine after the war. When Jewish terrorists murdered Lord Moyne in November 1944, Churchill warned the Zionists that friends such as himself would withdraw their support unless the Zionists themselves cooperated in stamping out terrorism.[6] By May 1945, with the war against Germany over, it had become apparent that the British government had no intention of establishing any kind of Jewish state in the foreseeable future. No Zionist leader could contem-

5. From July 1946 on, the British shipped all apprehended illegal immigrants to detention camps in Cyprus, essentially because the detention camps in Palestine had filled up, and because the British wanted to reassure the Arabs of their good intentions and to deter further Jewish immigration without permits.

6. On the Zionists' campaign against the terrorists (the so-called *saison*, or "hunting season"), see Michael J. Cohen, *Palestine: Retreat from the Mandate, 1936–1945* (New York, 1978); and Yehuda Bauer, *From Diplomacy to Resistance: A History of Jewish Palestine, 1939–1945* (Philadelphia, 1970).

plate cooperation with the British so long as the 1939 white paper remained the law of the land.

And so the British regime retreated behind its barbed-wire entanglements, watching the writ of British law gradually lose all authority. The climax of terrorist activity came at the end of July 1947, when the Irgun carried out its threat to execute two kidnapped British sergeants in revenge for the execution of several Irgun members. General revulsion in Britain provoked a wave of anti-Semitic disturbances, and a national consensus, articulated in Parliament, demanded the return of all British soldiers from Palestine.

And finally, there was the *Exodus* affair. In July 1947, with even the camps in Cyprus filled to overflowing with Jews, the government decided on a new policy of "*refoulement,*" returning illegal immigrants to their port of departure, back into the hands of the government that had allowed them to depart its territory. The *Exodus-1947,* carrying nearly 5,000 Jews, was the first ship to be subjected to the new policy. The ship was intercepted off the Palestine coast, *outside* territorial waters, and after a bloody battle was towed into Haifa. When the immigrants were taken back in British transports to the French port from which they had set out, they refused to disembark, and the French refused to take them off by force. After the immigrants had languished for weeks in the Mediterranean summer sun, suffering in abysmal sanitary conditions, the British were forced to send them to Hamburg, where they could provide both accommodation and the force to remove the Jews from the ships. The Jews saw to it that the whole pitiful affair, from Haifa to France to Hamburg, was carried out in the glare of the world media. It earned for Britain considerable international opprobrium, and for Bevin personally the odium of an inhuman monster.

The *Exodus* not only proved to be a considerable public relations success for the Jews, but it also signaled the inability of the British to cope with the ever-increasing flow of illegal immigrants to Palestine. By the end of 1947 the British had made a secret arrangement with the Jewish Agency to allow the overflow from the Cyprus camps surreptitiously back into Palestine.

The UN Partition Resolution, November 1947

In September 1947 Colonial Secretary Creech-Jones announced to the UN General Assembly that in the absence of a settlement in Palestine his government would withdraw its administration and armed forces. The British would not implement any solution, including partition, that was opposed by one of the sides. It was left to the Americans, whose president was on record as a supporter of the Zionist cause, to make their move.

Truman had kept aloof from the Palestine problem for nearly a year, since his Yom Kippur speech in October 1946. But if the United States could not now oppose the United Nations' endorsement of the Zionists' own program, this did not mean that the Americans would take the lead in sponsoring partition. The State Department was as concerned as the Foreign Office about negative Arab reactions and still considered it distinctly possible that the UN partition plan would not receive the required two-thirds majority vote in the General Assembly, since in September 1947 the Soviet Union and its satellites were still expected to vote against partition. It was recalled that in his speech the previous May, Andrei Gromyko, chief Soviet representative to the United Nations, had supported the Jews' claim to a state of their own, but only if the Soviets' first preference, a unitary Palestinian state, did not prove feasible.

American policy at the General Assembly was therefore to register formal support for partition, to demonstrate goodwill to the Arabs by seeking amendments in the proposed borders favorable to them, and, most important of all, to desist from exerting the influence the United States could so easily have exerted to persuade other delegations to vote for partition.

This strategy very nearly secured the State Department's goal of defeating partition. Although both the United States and the Soviet Union declared their support for partition (on 11 and 13 October, respectively), the first vote in the ad hoc committee on Palestine, on 25 November, did not produce the needed two-thirds majority (the vote was twenty-five in favor, thirteen against, with seventeen abstentions). The final vote in the General Assembly was due the next day, and it seemed as if the Zionist cause was doomed. So far, neither the conscience of the Western world nor the supposed sympathies of President Truman had secured for the Zionists the crucial international sanction for their claim to a state of their own. This they had to do for themselves.

Through a filibuster organized by their supporters, the Zionists secured an adjournment of the General Assembly. Because the following day was Thanksgiving, the Zionists in fact secured a forty-eight-hour interval in which to "influence" various delegations to change their vote. During these last forty-eight hours, the crucial influence of Truman himself, and of his White House, was finally brought into play. Presidential aides, ex–secretaries of state, members of Congress, and even Supreme Court justices joined together in an intensive lobby to secure more positive votes. When the vote was finally taken in the General Assembly on 29 November, seven of the delegations that had previously either opposed or abstained now voted in favor of partition, and the two-thirds majority was secured—thirty-three for, thirteen against, with ten abstentions.[7]

The Establishment of the State of Israel

The General Assembly vote gave rise to great rejoicing in the Yishuv, yet it by no means marked the end of the Zionists' struggles. The Arab world was determined to oppose the resolution with all the means at its disposal, and the Palestinians began a civil war on the day after its adoption. The Yishuv now had to prove to the world, and to the United States in particular, that it was sufficiently mature and able to grasp the opportunity that nationhood now held out. The British did not help matters by refusing to cooperate with the commission appointed by the United Nations to oversee the transfer of power to the successor states. Foreseeing that the Arabs would blame them for collusion with the UN attempt to impose partition on Palestine, the British refused the UN commission entry into Palestine until just two weeks before the end of the mandate.

Apprehensive of the risk to American interests in the Middle East resulting from U.S. support for partition in the General Assembly, the State Department immediately began a campaign to abort the UN resolution. The first step was the announcement in early December of an arms embargo on the Middle East. Such an embargo would obviously hurt the Jews most, for the Arabs, it was known, would continue to receive arms shipments under standing contracts with Britain.

7. See Cohen, *Palestine and the Great Powers,* pp. 292–300.

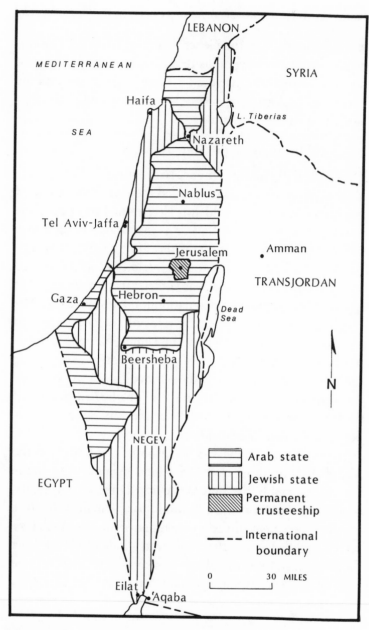

Map 5. The United Nations Partition Plan,
November 1947

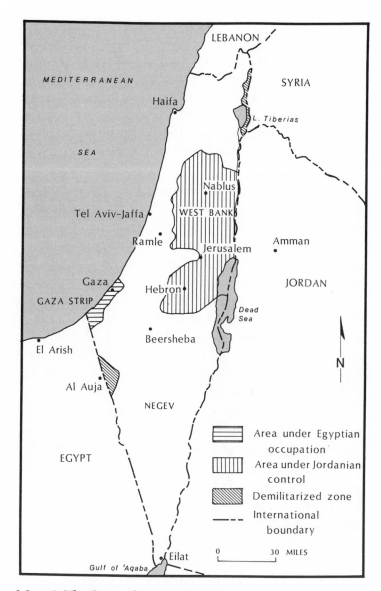

MEDITERRANEAN

SEA

LEBANON

SYRIA

Haifa

L. Tiberias

Nablus

Tel Aviv-Jaffa

WEST BANK

Ramle

Jerusalem

Amman

Gaza

JORDAN

GAZA STRIP

Hebron

Dead
Sea

Beersheba

El Arish

Al Auja

NEGEV

N

EGYPT

Area under Egyptian
occupation

Area under Jordanian
control

Demilitarized zone

International
boundary

0   30 MILES

Eilat

Gulf of 'Aqaba

Map 6. The State of Israel, 1949–1967

The State Department stressed also that the UN resolution was merely a *recommendation* predicated on a peaceful transition process and on economic union between the two successor states. The resolution had certainly not taken into account a civil war, a conflict that might possibly spread beyond the borders of Palestine and attract great power intervention.

As the State Department developed its case during the first months of 1948, East-West relations in Europe deteriorated seriously. In February there was a communist coup in Czechoslovakia, and on 5 March the military governor of the American Zone in Berlin, General Lucius Clay, sent his famous telegram warning that war with the Soviet Union might come at any time; indeed, shortly afterward, the Soviets began hindering the Allies' traffic to Berlin, whose land approaches were soon effectively blockaded. With military alerts sounding in Europe, the Americans could not afford to allow Palestine to drift into chaos, thereby providing a further theater for Soviet advance.

Not only was security in Palestine disappearing, but during the first phase of the war the Jews also seemed to be getting decisively the worst of the battle. Many of the Yishuv's staunchest supporters inclined to a State Department plan to defer statehood and place Palestine under international supervision, if only to save the Jewish community from physical annihilation. Many Jewish settlements, and indeed Jerusalem itself, were besieged by the Arabs, who were winning the "battle of communications." The Jewish Agency was advised by military experts to withdraw to the coastal plain, concentrating its defenses there instead of dispersing them across the country. But any withdrawal would have had permanent consequences, at best ultimate confinement to a puppet state along the coast. So orthodox military doctrine was overruled by high policy.

By March 1948 the Zionists' fortunes, both political and military, had sunk to their nadir. At the Security Council the Americans proposed that the UN resolution on Palestine be shelved and that the country be governed by some form of international trusteeship until conditions there permitted the granting of independence.

But now the tide of military fortune turned in Palestine. At the end of March the Jews received their first shipment of heavy arms, flown in clandestinely from Czechoslovakia. The Hagana went on the offensive and, in a series of operations carried out from early April until mid-May, successfully consolidated and created communication links with all those Jewish settlements designated by the United Nations to become the Jewish state. The siege of Jerusalem was also lifted, albeit only temporarily.

In the meantime, the Americans' trusteeship plan secured little support at the United Nations, mainly owing to their reluctance to commit their own forces. The Jews, Arabs, and British all refused to consider the plan seriously.

With the Jews establishing their state de facto in Palestine, the endless debates at Lake Success became more academic and less related to reality. Had the State Department plan to implement trusteeship been carried through, it would have been necessary to act with force against the UN resolution of the previous November.

On 14 May 1948, in one of the strangest scenes ever witnessed at the United Nations, news of President Truman's de facto recognition of the state of Israel came over the ticker tapes at the very moment the American delegates were pressing the trusteeship proposals. Truman, out of a mixture of self-interest and political common sense, decided to recognize the facts and reap what benefits could still be extracted from a volatile situation. With no force in the world ready or able to prevent the establishment of the Jewish state, and with rumors that the Soviet Union was about to recognize it, Truman threw caution and diplomatic etiquette to the winds and once more asserted his own personal brand of presidential prerogative.

For the Zionists, military triumph brought the reward of diplomatic recognition. For the Palestinian Arabs, the disunity of the Arab world and, perhaps above all, lack of internal cohesion and a dearth of administrative or military skills brought disaster.

Documents

Negib Azouri, Program of the League
of the Arab Fatherland

Extract from Reveil de la nation arabe dans l'Asie turque
. . . (Paris, 1905) translated by Sylvia G. Haim and re-
produced from her Arab Nationalism: An Anthology
(Berkeley and Los Angeles, 1962), pp. 81–82. Azouri
was a Christian Arab who lived for long periods in Paris
and tried in vain to interest France and Britain in his pro-
gram for Arab independence.

. . . There is nothing more liberal than the league's program. The league wants, before anything else, to separate
the civil and the religious power, in the interest of Islam
and the Arab nation, and to form an Arab empire stretch-
ing from the Tigris and the Euphrates to the Suez Isthmus,
and from the Mediterranean to the Arabian Sea.

The mode of government will be a constitutional sul-
tanate based on the freedom of all the religions and the
equality of all the citizens before the law. It will respect the
interests of Europe, all the concessions and all the privileges which had been granted to her up to now by the

Turks. It will also respect the autonomy of the Lebanon, and the independence of the principalities of Yemen, Nejd, and Iraq.

The league offers the throne of the Arab Empire to that prince of the Khedivial family of Egypt who will openly declare himself in its favor and who will devote his energy and his resources to this end.

It rejects the idea of unifying Egypt and the Arab Empire under the same monarchy, because the Egyptians do not belong to the Arab race; they are of the African Berber family and the language which they spoke before Islam bears no similarity to Arabic. There exists, moreover, between Egypt and the Arab Empire a natural frontier which must be respected in order to avoid the introduction, in the new state, of the germs of discord and destruction. Never, as a matter of fact, have the ancient Arab caliphs succeeded for any length of time in controlling the two countries at the same time. . . .

Theodor Herzl, Extract from *The Jewish State*

Herzl, the founder of modern political Zionism, published Der Judenstaat *in Vienna in 1896.*

. . . The Jewish question still exists. It would be foolish to deny it. It is a remnant of the Middle Ages, which civilized nations do not even yet seem able to shake off, try as they will. They certainly showed a generous desire to do so when they emancipated us. The Jewish question exists wherever Jews live in perceptible numbers. Where it does not exist, it is carried by Jews in the course of their migrations. We naturally move to those places where we are not persecuted, and there our presence produces persecution. This is the case in every country, and will remain so, even in those highly civilized—for instance, France—until the Jewish question finds a solution on a political basis. The unfortunate Jews are now carrying the seeds of Anti-Semitism into England; they have already introduced it into America. . . .

No one can deny the gravity of the situation of the Jews. Wherever they live in perceptible numbers, they are more or less persecuted. Their equality before the law, granted by statute, has become practically a dead letter. They are debarred from filling even moderately high positions, either in the army, or in any public or private capacity. And attempts are made to thrust them out of business also: "Don't buy from Jews!"

Attacks in Parliaments, in assemblies, in the press, in the pulpit, in the street, on journeys—for example, their exclusion from certain hotels—even in places of recreation, become daily more numerous. The forms of persecutions varying according to the countries and social circles in which they occur. In Russia, imposts are levied on Jewish villages; in Rumania, a few persons are put to death; in Germany, they get a good beating occasionally; in Austria, Anti-Semites exercise terrorism over all public life; in Algeria, there are travelling agitators; in Paris, the Jews are shut out of the so-called best social circles and excluded from clubs. Shades of anti-Jewish feeling are innumerable. But this is not to be an attempt to make out a doleful category of Jewish hardships. . . .

The Plan

The whole plan is in its essence perfectly simple, as it must necessarily be if it is to come within the comprehension of all.

Let the sovereignty be granted us over a portion of the globe large enough to satisfy the rightful requirements of a nation; the rest we shall manage for ourselves.

The creation of a new State is neither ridiculous nor impossible. We have in our day witnessed the process in connection with nations which were not largely members of the middle class, but poorer, less educated, and consequently weaker than ourselves. The Governments of all countries scourged by Anti-Semitism will be keenly interested in assisting us to obtain the sovereignty we want.

The plan, simple in design, but complicated in execution, will be carried out by two agencies: The Society of Jews and the Jewish Company.

The Society of Jews will do the preparatory work in the domains of science and politics, which the Jewish Company will afterwards apply practically.

The Jewish Company will be the liquidating agent of the business interests of departing Jews, and will organize commerce and trade in the new country.

We must not imagine the departure of the Jews to be a sudden one. It will be gradual, continuous, and will cover many decades. The poorest will go first to cultivate the soil. In accordance with a preconceived plan, they will construct roads, bridges, railways and telegraph installations; regulate rivers; and build their own dwellings; their labor will create trade, trade will create markets and markets will attract new settlers, for every man will go voluntarily, at his own expense and his own risk. The labor expended on the land will enhance its value, and the Jews will soon perceive that a new and permanent sphere of operation is opening here for that spirit of enterprise which has heretofore met only with hatred and obloquy. . . .

Should the Powers declare themselves willing to admit

our sovereignty over a neutral piece of land, then the Society will enter into negotiations for the possession of this land. Here two territories come under consideration, Palestine and Argentine. In both countries important experiments in colonization have been made, though on the mistaken principle of a gradual infiltration of Jews. An infiltration is bound to end badly. It continues till the inevitable moment when the native population feels itself threatened, and forces the Government to stop a further influx of Jews. Immigration is consequently futile unless we have the sovereign right to continue such immigration.

The Society of Jews will treat with the present masters of the land, putting itself under the protectorate of the European Powers, if they prove friendly to the plan. We could offer the present possessors of the land enormous advantages, assume part of the public debt, build new roads for traffic, which our presence in the country would render necessary, and do many other things. The creation of our State would be beneficial to adjacent countries, because the cultivation of a strip of land increases the value of its surrounding districts in innumerable ways. . . .

Arab Nationalist Manifesto, Cairo, 1914

Reproduced from Sylvia G. Haim, Arab Nationalism: An Anthology *(Berkeley and Los Angeles, 1962), pp. 83–87.*

Announcement to the Arabs, Sons of Qahtan

O Sons of Qahtan! O Descendants of Adnan! Are you asleep? And how long will you remain asleep? How can you remain deep in your slumber when the voices of the nations around you have deafened everyone? Do you not hear the commotion all around you? Do you not know that you live in a period when he who sleeps dies, and he who dies is gone forever? When will you open your eyes and see the glitter of the bayonets which are directed at you, and the lightning of the swords which are drawn over your heads? When will you realize the truth? When will you know that your country has been sold to the foreigner? See how your natural resources have been alienated from you and have come into the possession of England, France, and Germany. . . .

Arise, O ye Arabs! Unsheathe the sword from the scabbard, ye sons of Qahtan! Do not allow an oppressive tyrant who has only disdain for you to remain in your country; cleanse your country from those who show their enmity to you, to your race and to your language. . . .

O ye Muslim Arabs, you make a great mistake if you think that this tyrannical, lawless government is Islamic. God says in His precious Book: the unbelievers are the tyrants.

Every tyrannical government is an enemy and a foe to Islam; how more so, then, if the government destroys Islam, considers it lawful to shed the blood of the people of the Prophet of Islam, and seeks to kill the language of Islam in the name of Islamic government and the Islamic caliphate? He who seeks proof has only to read the book *A New Nation* by Ubaidullah, the creature of the unionists, a book which they have used as one of the preliminaries for the destruction of Islam. Therefore, he who supports these unionists because he considers them Muslims is in clear error, for none of them have done a good deed for Islam. Indeed, most of them have no root in that Turkism for the sake of which they are fighting the Koran. They are merely Turks by virtue of this counterfeit language they speak, which derives what is best in it from the sacred Arabic tongue and the sweet Persian tongue. Fanatic in its cause, they fight the Koran and the tradition of the Arabic Prophet. Is this the Islam which it is incumbent on them to respect? It is not notorious that they seek to kill the Arabic language? Did they not write books to show that it must be abandoned, and that prayers and the call to prayers should be made in Turkish? And if Arabic dies, how can the Koran and the traditions live? And if the Book and the traditions cease to be known, what remains of Islam?

And O ye Christian and Jewish Arabs, combine with your brethren the Muslim Arabs, and do not follow in the footsteps of him who says to you, whether he be one of you or not: The Arab Muslims are sunk in religious fanaticism, therefore we prefer the irreligious Turks. This is nonsensical speech which proceeds from an ignorant man who knows neither his own nor his people's interest. The Muslim Arabs are your brethren in patriotism, and if you find among them some who are seized with an ugly fanaticism, so likewise are such to be found among you. Both sides, indeed, have learnt it from the non-Arabs. Our ancestors were not fanatical in this sense, for Jews and Christians used to study in the mosques of Baghdad and the Andalus like brethren. Let them, both sides, aim at tolerance. . . .

Sir Henry McMahon to Sharif Husayn, 24 October 1915

The entire correspondence was published in English first by George Antonius, The Arab Awakening *(London, 1938), and next in a British white paper, Cmd. 5957, March 1939. (See Map 1, p. 21.)*

. . . The two districts of Mersina and Alexandretta and portions of Syria lying to the west of the districts of Damascus, Homs, Hama and Aleppo cannot be said to be purely Arab, and should be excluded from the limits demanded.

With the above modification, and without prejudice to our existing treaties with Arab chiefs, we accept those limits.

As for those regions lying within those frontiers wherein Great Britain is free to act without detriment to the interests of her ally, France, I am empowered in the name of the Government of Great Britain to give the following assurances and make the following reply to your letter:

(1) Subject to the above modifications, Great Britain is prepared to recognise and support the independence of the Arabs in all the regions within the limits demanded by the Sherif of Mecca.

(2) Great Britain will guarantee the Holy Places against all external aggression and will recognise their inviolability.

(3) When the situation admits, Great Britain will give to the Arabs her advice and will assist them to establish what may appear to be the most suitable forms of government in those various territories.

(4) On the other hand, it is understood that the Arabs have decided to seek the advice and guidance of Great Britain only, and that such European advisers and officials as may be required for the formation of a sound form of administration will be British.

(5) With regard to the *vilayets* of Bagdad and Basra, the Arabs will recognise that the established position and interests of Great Britain necessitate special administrative arrangements in order to secure these territories from foreign aggression to promote the welfare of the local populations and to safeguard our mutual economic interests.

The Sykes-Picot Agreement, May 1916

Articles 1 and 11 refer apparently to the Husayn-McMahon correspondence and would indicate therefore an attempt to take into account the British commitment to Arab independence. (See Map 2, p. 43.)

Grey to Cambon, 16 May 1916

I have the honour to acknowledge the receipt of your Excellency's note of the 9th instant, stating that the French Government accept the limits of a future Arab State, or Confederation of States, and of those parts of Syria where French interests predominate, together with certain conditions attached thereto, such as they result from recent discussions in London and Petrograd on the subject.

I have the honour to inform your Excellency in reply that the acceptance of the whole project, as it now stands, will involve the abdication of considerable British interests, but, since His Majesty's Government recognise the advantage to the general cause of the Allies entailed in producing a more favourable internal political situation in Turkey, they are ready to accept the arrangement now arrived at, provided that the co-operation of the Arabs is secured, and that the Arabs fulfil the conditions and obtain the towns of Homs, Hama, Damascus, and Aleppo.

It is accordingly understood between the French and British Governments—

1. That France and Great Britain are prepared to recognise and protect an independent Arab State or a Confederation of Arab States in the areas (A) and (B) . . . under the suzerainty of an Arab chief. That in area (A) France, and in area (B) Great Britain, shall have priority of right of enterprise and local loans. That in area (A) France, and in

area (B) Great Britain, shall alone supply advisers or foreign functionaries at the request of the Arab State or Confederation of Arab States.

2. That in the blue area France, and in the red area Great Britain, shall be allowed to establish such direct or indirect administration or control as they desire and as they may think fit to arrange with the Arab State or Confederation of Arab States.

3. That in the brown area there shall be established an international administration, the form of which is to be decided upon after consultation with Russia, and subsequently in consultation with the other Allies, and the representatives of the Shereef of Mecca. . . .

10. The British and French Governments, as the protectors of the Arab State, shall agree that they will not themselves acquire and will not consent to a third Power acquiring territorial possessions in the Arabian peninsula, nor consent to a third Power installing a naval base either on the east coast, or on the islands, of the Red Sea. This, however, shall not prevent such adjustment of the Aden frontier as may be necessary in consequence of recent Turkish aggression.

11. The negotiations with the Arabs as to the boundaries of the Arab State or Confederation of Arab States shall be continued through the same channel as heretofore on behalf of the two Powers. . . .

The Balfour Declaration, 2 November 1917

Foreign Secretary Arthur Balfour sent the British government's revised statement to Lord Rothschild, head of the

Anglo-Jewish community. The British commitment was not intended to be kept secret, and it was widely published in the press (though censored by the British military authorities in Palestine).

Official Zionist Formula, 18 July 1917

H.M. Government, after considering the aims of the Zionist Organisation, accepts the principle of recognising Palestine as the National Home of the Jewish people and the right of the Jewish people to build up its National life in Palestine under a protection to be established at the conclusion of Peace, following upon the successful issue of the war.

H.M. Government regards as essential for the realisation of this principle the grant of internal autonomy to the Jewish nationality in Palestine, freedom of immigration for Jews, and the establishment of a Jewish National Colonising Corporation for the re-settlement and economic development of the country.

The conditions and forms of the internal autonomy and a charter for the Jewish National Colonising Corporation should, in the view of H.M. Government, be elaborated in detail and determined with the representatives of the Zionist Organisation.

The Balfour Declaration, 2 November 1917

I have much pleasure in conveying to you on behalf of his Majesty's Government, the following declaration of sympathy with Jewish Zionist aspirations which has been submitted to and approved by the Cabinet:—

His Majesty's Government view with favour the establishment in Palestine of a national home for the Jewish people, and will use their best endeavours to facilitate the achievement of this object, it being clearly understood that nothing shall be done which may prejudice the civil and religious rights of existing non-Jewish communities in Palestine, or the rights and political status enjoyed by Jews in any other country.

I should be grateful if you would bring this declaration to the knowledge of the Zionist Federation.

The Faysal-Weizmann Agreement, 3 January 1919

The agreement, signed in Paris on the eve of the peace conference, was apparently not communicated to the Syrian nationalists, much less to the Arabs living in Palestine. By the terms of Faysal's handwritten reservation, the agreement automatically became null and void when Faysal was ousted from Syria by the French in July 1920. Subsequently, as king of Iraq, Faysal denied all knowledge of the agreement.

Agreement Between Emir Feisal and Dr. Weizmann, January 3, 1919

His Royal Highness the Emir Feisal, representing and acting on behalf of the Arab Kingdom of Hedjaz, and Dr. Chaim Weizmann, representing and acting on behalf of the Zionist Organisation, mindful of the racial kinship and ancient bonds existing between the Arabs and the Jewish people, and realising that the surest means of working out the consummation of their national aspirations is through the closest possible collaboration in the development of the Arab State and Palestine, and being desirous further of confirming the good understanding which exists between them, have agreed upon the following Articles:

ARTICLE I

The Arab State and Palestine in all their relations and undertakings shall be controlled by the most cordial goodwill and understanding, and to this end Arab and Jewish duly accredited agents shall be established and maintained in the respective territories.

ARTICLE II

Immediately following the completion of the deliberations of the Peace Conference, the definite boundaries between the Arab State and Palestine shall be determined by a Commission to be agreed upon by the parties hereto.

ARTICLE III

In the establishment of the Constitution and Administration of Palestine all such measures shall be adopted as will afford the fullest guarantees for carrying into effect the British Government's Declaration of the 2d of November, 1917.

ARTICLE IV

All necessary measures shall be taken to encourage and stimulate immigration of Jews into Palestine on a large scale, and as quickly as possible to settle Jewish immigrants upon the land through closer settlement and intensive cultivation of the soil. In taking such measures the Arab peasant and tenant farmers shall be protected in their rights, and shall be assisted in forwarding their economic development.

ARTICLE V

No regulation nor law shall be made prohibiting or interfering in any way with the free exercise of religion; and further the free exercise and enjoyment of religious profession and worship without discrimination or reference shall forever be allowed. No religious test shall ever be required for the exercise of civil or political rights.

ARTICLE VI

The Mohammedan Holy Places shall be under Mohammedan control.

ARTICLE VII

The Zionist Organisation proposes to send to Palestine a Commission of experts to make a survey of the economic possibilities of the country, and to report upon the best means for its development. The Zionist Organisation will place the aforementioned Commission at the disposal of the Arab State for the purpose of a survey of the economic possibilities of the Arab State and to report upon the best means for its development. The Zionist Organisation will use its best efforts to assist the Arab State in providing the means for developing the natural resources and economic possibilities thereof.

ARTICLE VIII

The parties hereto agree to act in complete accord and harmony on all matters embraced herein before the Peace Congress.

ARTICLE IX

Any matters of dispute which may arise between the contracting parties shall be referred to the British Government for arbitration.

Given under our hand at London, England, the third day of January, one thousand nine hundred and nineteen.

CHAIM WEIZMANN
FEISAL IBN-HUSSEIN

[Handwritten] Reservation by the Emir Feisal

If the Arabs are established as I have asked in my manifesto of January 4th addressed to the British Secretary of State for Foreign Affairs, I will carry out what is written in this agreement. If changes are made, I cannot be answerable for failing to carry out this agreement.

FEISAL IBN-HUSSEIN

Extract from the 1922 (Churchill) White Paper, Cmd. 1700, July 1922

The tension which has prevailed from time to time in Palestine is mainly due to apprehensions, which are entertained both by sections of the Arab and by sections of the Jewish population. These apprehensions, so far as the Arabs are concerned, are partly based upon exaggerated interpretations of the meaning of the Declaration favouring the establishment of a Jewish National Home in Palestine, made on behalf of His Majesty's Government on 2nd November, 1917. Unauthorised statements have been made to the effect that the purpose in view is to create a wholly Jewish Palestine. Phrases have been used such as that Palestine is to become "as Jewish as England is English." His Majesty's Government regard any such expectation as impracticable and have no such aim in view. Nor have they at any time contemplated, as appears to be feared by the Arab Delegation, the disappearance or the subordination of the Arabic population, language or culture in Palestine. They would draw attention to the fact that the terms of the Declaration referred to do not contemplate that Palestine as a whole should be converted into a Jewish National Home, but that such a Home should be founded *in Palestine*. . . .

When it is asked what is meant by the development of the Jewish National Home in Palestine, it may be answered that it is not the imposition of a Jewish nationality upon the inhabitants of Palestine as a whole, but the further development of the existing Jewish community, with the assistance of Jews in other parts of the world, in order that it may become a centre in which the Jewish people as a whole may take, on grounds of religion and race, an interest and a pride. But in order that this community should have the best prospect of free development and provide a full opportunity for the Jewish people to display its capacities, it is essential that it should know that it is in Palestine as of right and not on sufferance. That is the reason why it is necessary that the existence of a Jewish National Home in Palestine should be internationally guaranteed, and that it should be formally recognised to rest upon ancient historic connection. . . .

For the fulfilment of this policy it is necessary that the Jewish community in Palestine should be able to increase its numbers by immigration. This immigration cannot be so great in volume as to exceed whatever may be the economic capacity of the country at the time to absorb new arrivals. It is essential to ensure that the immigrants should not be a burden upon the people of Palestine as a whole, and that they should not deprive any section of the present population of their employment. Hitherto the immigration has fulfilled these conditions. . . .

With reference to the Constitution which it is now intended to establish in Palestine, the draft of which has already been published, it is desirable to make certain points clear. In the first place, it is not the case, as has been represented by the Arab Delegation, that during the war His Majesty's Government gave an undertaking that an independent national government should be at once established in Palestine. This representation mainly rests upon a letter dated the 24th October, 1915, from Sir Henry McMahon, then His Majesty's High Commissioner in Egypt, to the Sherif of Mecca, now King Hussein of the Kingdom of the Hejaz. That letter is quoted as conveying the promise to the Sherif of Mecca to recognise and support the independence of the Arabs within the territories proposed by him. But this promise was given subject to a reservation made in the same letter, which excluded from its scope, among other territories, the portions of Syria lying to the west of the district of Damascus. This reservation has always been regarded by His Majesty's Government as covering the vilayet of Beirut and the independent Sanjak of Jerusalem. The whole of Palestine west of the Jordan was thus excluded from Sir H. McMahon's pledge.

Nevertheless, it is the intention of His Majesty's Government to foster the establishment of a full measure of self-government in Palestine. But they are of opinion that, in the special circumstances of that country, this should be accomplished by gradual stages and not suddenly. The first step was taken when, on the institution of a civil Administration, the nominated Advisory Council, which now exists, was established. It was stated at the time by the High Commissioner that this was the first step in the development of self-governing institutions, and it is now proposed to take a second step by the establishment of a Legislative Council containing a large proportion of members elected on a wide franchise. . . .

Winston S. Churchill (Colonial Secretary), Speech on
"Zionism and Palestine," 4 July 1922

Parliamentary Debates *(Commons), 5th ser., vol. 156, cols. 327–342.*

Broadly speaking, there are two issues raised to-night, and it is very important to keep them distinct. The first is, Are we to keep our pledge to the Zionists made in 1917 to the effect that His Majesty's Government would use their best endeavours to facilitate the achievement of a National Home for the Jewish people? Are we to keep that pledge or are we to abandon it? That is the first issue. The second issue is a separate one, and it is: Are the measures taken by the Colonial Office to fulfil that pledge reasonable and proper measures? That is a different question, and I think the Committee is in a very different position with regard to each of those two issues. It is entirely at liberty to criticise the administration of the Colonial Office. If that administration has been wrongly conceived or ill-directed; if it is marked by improper incidents; if it is not, in fact, a reasonable and proper way of carrying out the policy of Great Britain, this is the time to expose it, this is the time to inflict Parliamentary censure upon the Minister and the Department responsible.

With regard to the larger issue of whether we should or should not repudiate our promise to the Zionists, I venture to suggest the Committee has not the same freedom. No doubt individual Members who have always opposed the Zionist policy—if such there be—are perfectly consistent in opposing it now, but the House, as a whole, has definitely committed itself on more than one occasion to the general proposition that we should use our best endeavours to make good our pledges and facilitate the achievement of a National Home for the Jewish people in Palestine. There never has been any serious challenge to that policy in Parliament. Pledges and promises were made during the War, and they were made, not only on the merits, though I think the merits are considerable. They were made because it was considered they would be of value to us in our struggle to win the War. It was considered that the support which the Jews could give us all over the world, and particularly in the United States, and also in Russia, would be a definite palpable advantage. I was not responsible at that time for the giving of those pledges, nor for the conduct of the War of which they were, when given, an integral part. But like other Members I supported the policy of the War Cabinet. . . .

. . . There is no doubt whatever that the fulfilment of the Balfour Declaration was an integral part of the whole mandatory system, as inaugurated by agreement between the victorious Powers and by the Treaty of Versailles. These are decisions in which I have taken only a very subordinate part, and which the House at every stage has approved. And speaking as Colonial Secretary, charged with the execution of a particular policy, a policy adopted and confirmed by this country before the whole world, I am bound by the pledges and promises which have been given in the name of Great Britain in the past, and by the decisions which Parliament has taken from time to time. . . .

You have no right to say this kind of thing as individuals; you have no right to support public declarations made in the name of your country in the crisis and heat of the War, and then afterwards, when all is cold and prosaic, to turn round and attack the Minister or the Department which is faithfully and laboriously endeavouring to translate these perfervid enthusiasms into the sober, concrete facts of day-to-day administration. . . .

We really must know where we are. Who led us along
this path, who impelled us along it? I remained quite silent.
I am not in the "Black Book." I accepted service on the
lines laid down for me. Now, when I am endeavouring to
carry it out, it is from this quarter that I am assailed.

I am bound to ask the Committee to take the vote which
is about to be given as a vote of confidence, because we
cannot carry out our pledges to the Zionists, with which
the House is fully familiar, unless we are permitted to use
Jews, and use Jews freely, within what limits are proper, to
develop new sources of wealth in Palestine. I am bound
also to ask the Committee to attach significance to this vote
because of the adverse vote recorded in another place a few
days ago. I think that it was a very unfortunate vote. As far
as this House and the country are concerned, it does not
make much difference. We all know that you can easily get
60 or 70 Members of that Chamber together. We all remember the vote given on the subject of Miss Violet Douglas-
Pennant. This vote may have a serious result in Palestine. It
might lead to violent disturbances, and though we consider
ourselves properly equipped to deal with such disturbances,
and have every intention of putting them down with a firm
hand, a vote like this, unless dealt with by the House of
Commons, might lead to distress and bloodshed. We are
doing our best to carry out the pledges as entered into both
to the Jews and the Arabs. We are doing our best to develop
the resources of Palestine in order to recoup the expenditure
made by this country. The year before last we were faced
with a cost of £8,000,000; last year it cost £4,000,000; this
year it was estimated at a cost of £2,000,000. I had long
talks with Sir Herbert Samuel while he was over here.
He promised me that next year it will not be more than
£1,500,000, and the year after that only £1,000,000.

This is a great reduction in four years of administration—from £8,000,000 to £1,000,000. I say that Palestine is all the more important to us in view of what is happening, in view of the ever-growing significance to the British Empire of the Suez Canal; and I do not think £1,000,000 a year, even if further reductions cannot be obtained—and I do not admit that no further reductions can be obtained—would be too much for Great Britain to pay for the control and guardianship of this great historic land, and for keeping the word she has given before all the nations of the world. . . .

The Royal Commission (Peel) Report, Cmd. 5479, July 1937

(See Map 4, p. 94.)

. . . For Partition means that neither will get all it wants. It means that the Arabs must acquiesce in the exclusion from their sovereignty of a piece of territory, long occupied and once ruled by them. It means that the Jews must be content with less than the Land of Israel they once ruled and have hoped to rule again. But it seems to us possible that on reflection both parties will come to realize that the drawbacks of Partition are outweighed by its advantages. For, if it offers neither party all it wants, it offers each what it wants most, namely freedom and security.

2. The advantages to the Arabs of Partition on the lines we have proposed may be summarized as follows:

(i) They obtain their national independence and can cooperate on an equal footing with the Arabs of the neighbouring countries in the cause of Arab unity and progress.

(ii) They are finally delivered from the fear of being "swamped" by the Jews and from the possibility of ultimate subjection to Jewish rule.

(iii) In particular, the final limitation of the Jewish National Home within a fixed frontier and the enactment of a new Mandate for the protection of the Holy Places, solemnly guaranteed by the League of Nations, removes all anxiety lest the Holy Places should ever come under Jewish control.

(iv) As a set-off to the loss of territory the Arabs regard as theirs, the Arab State will receive a subvention from the Jewish State. It will also, in view of the backwardness of Trans-Jordan, obtain a grant of £2,000,000 from the British Treasury; and, if an arrangement can be made for the exchange of land and population, a further grant will be made for the conversion, as far as may prove possible, of uncultivable land in the Arab State into productive land from which the cultivators and the State alike will profit.

3. The advantages of Partition to the Jews may be summarized as follows:

(i) Partition secures the establishment of the Jewish National Home and relieves it from the possibility of its being subjected in the future to Arab rule.

(ii) Partition enables the Jews in the fullest sense to call their National Home their own: for it converts it into a Jewish State. Its citizens will be able to admit as many Jews into it as they themselves believe can be absorbed. They will attain the primary objective of Zionism—a Jewish nation, planted in Palestine, giving its nationals the same status in the world as other nations give theirs. They will cease at last to live a "minority life."

Palestine White Paper, Cmd. 6019, 17 May 1939

Only the constitutional and immigration provisions are extracted here. Restrictions on Jewish land purchases were promulgated in February 1940.

. . . His Majesty's Government make the following declaration of their intentions regarding the future government of Palestine:—

(1) The objective of His Majesty's Government is the establishment within ten years of an independent Palestine State in such treaty relations with the United Kingdom as will provide satisfactorily for the commercial and strategic requirements of both countries in the future. This proposal for the establishment of the independent State would involve consultation with the Council of the League of Nations with a view to the termination of the Mandate.

(2) The independent State should be one in which Arabs and Jews share in government in such a way as to ensure that the essential interests of each community are safeguarded.

(3) The establishment of the independent State will be preceded by a transitional period throughout which His Majesty's Government will retain responsibility for the government of the country. During the transitional period the people of Palestine will be given an increasing part in the government of their country. Both sections of the population will have an opportunity to participate in the machinery of government, and the process will be carried on whether or not they both avail themselves of it.

(4) As soon as peace and order have been sufficiently restored in Palestine steps will be taken to carry out this policy of giving the people of Palestine an increasing part in the government of their country, the objective being to

place Palestinians in charge of all the Departments of Government, with the assistance of British advisers and subject to the control of the High Commissioner. With this object in view His Majesty's Government will be prepared immediately to arrange that Palestinians shall be placed in charge of certain Departments, with British advisers. . . .

(6) At the end of five years from the restoration of peace and order, an appropriate body representative of the people of Palestine and of His Majesty's Government will be set up to review the working of the constitutional arrangements during the transitional period and to consider and make recommendations regarding the constitution of the independent Palestine State.

(7) His Majesty's Government will require to be satisfied that in the treaty contemplated by sub-paragraph (1) or in the constitution contemplated by sub-paragraph (6) adequate provision has been made for:—

(a) the security of, and freedom of access to, the Holy Places, and the protection of the interests and property of the various religious bodies.

(b) the protection of the different communities in Palestine in accordance with the obligations of His Majesty's Government to both Arabs and Jews and for the special position in Palestine of the Jewish National Home.

(c) such requirements to meet the strategic situation as may be regarded as necessary by His Majesty's Government in the light of the circumstances then existing. . . .

(8) His Majesty's Government will do everything in their power to create conditions which will enable the independent Palestine State to come into being within ten years. If, at the end of ten years, it appears to His Majesty's Government that, contrary to their hope, circumstances re-

quire the postponement of the establishment of the independent State, they will consult with representatives of the people of Palestine, the Council of the League of Nations and the neighbouring Arab States before deciding on such a postponement. . . .

14. (1) Jewish immigration during the next five years will be at a rate which, if economic absorptive capacity permits, will bring the Jewish population up to approximately one-third of the total population of the country. Taking into account the expected natural increase of the Arab and Jewish populations, and the number of illegal Jewish immigrants now in the country, this would allow of the admission, as from the beginning of April this year, of some 75,000 immigrants over the next five years. These immigrants would, subject to the criterion of economic absorptive capacity, be admitted as follows:

(a) For each of the next five years a quota of 10,000 Jewish immigrants will be allowed, on the understanding that a shortage in any one year may be added to the quotas for subsequent years, within the five-year period, if economic absorptive capacity permits.

(b) In addition, as a contribution towards the solution of the Jewish refugee problem, 25,000 refugees will be admitted as soon as the High Commissioner is satisfied that adequate provision for their maintenance is ensured, special consideration being given to refugee children and dependants.

(2) The existing machinery for ascertaining economic absorptive capacity will be retained, and the High Commissioner will have the ultimate responsibility for deciding the limits of economic capacity. Before each periodic decision is taken, Jewish and Arab representatives will be consulted.

(3) After the period of five years no further Jewish immigration will be permitted unless the Arabs of Palestine are prepared to acquiesce in it.

(4) His Majesty's Government are determined to check illegal immigration, and further preventive measures are being adopted. The numbers of any Jewish illegal immigrants who, despite these measures, may succeed in coming into the country and cannot be deported will be deducted from the yearly quotas.

15. His Majesty's Government are satisfied that, when the immigration over five years which is now contemplated has taken place, they will not be justified in facilitating, nor will they be under any obligation to facilitate, the further development of the Jewish National Home by immigration regardless of the wishes of the Arab population. . . .

Pact of the Arab League, 22 March 1945: Annex Relating to Palestine

(1) *Annex Regarding Palestine.* Since the termination of the last great war the rule of the Ottoman Empire over the Arab countries, among them Palestine, which had become detached from that Empire, has come to an end. She has come to be independent in herself, not subordinate to any other state.

The Treaty of Lausanne proclaimed that her future was to be settled by the parties concerned.

However, even though she was as yet unable to control her own affairs, the Covenant of the League (of Nations) in 1919 made provision for a regime based upon recognition of her independence.

Her international existence and independence in the legal sense cannot, therefore, be questioned, any more than could the independence of the other Arab countries.

Although the outward manifestations of this independence have remained obscured for reasons beyond her control, this should not be allowed to interfere with her participation in the work of the Council of the League.

The States signatory to the Pact of the Arab League are therefore of the opinion that, considering the special circumstances of Palestine, and until that country can effectively exercise its independence, the Council of the League should take charge of the selection of an Arab representative from Palestine to take part in its work. . . .

Report of the Anglo-American Committee on Palestine and Related Problems, Cmd. 6808, 20 April 1946

Recommendation No. 1.   We have to report that such information as we received about countries other than Palestine gave no hope of substantial assistance in finding homes for Jews wishing or impelled to leave Europe.

But Palestine alone cannot meet the emigration needs of the Jewish victims of Nazi and Fascist persecution; the whole world shares responsibility for them and indeed for the resettlement of all "displaced persons."

We therefore recommend that our Governments together, and in association with other countries, should endeavor immediately to find new homes for all such "displaced persons," irrespective of creed or nationality, whose ties with their former communities have been irreparably broken.

Though emigration will solve the problems of some victims of persecution, the overwhelming majority, including a considerable number of Jews, will continue to live in Europe. We recommend therefore that our Governments endeavor to secure that immediate effect is given to the provision of the United Nations Charter calling for "universal respect for, and observance of, human rights and fundamental freedoms for all without distinction as to race, sex, language, or religion." . . .

Recommendation No. 2. We recommend *(a)* that 100,000 certificates be authorized immediately for the admission into Palestine of Jews who have been the victims of Nazi and Fascist persecution; *(b)* that these certificates be awarded as far as possible in 1946 and that actual immigration be pushed forward as rapidly as conditions will permit. . . .

Recommendation No. 3. In order to dispose, once and for all, of the exclusive claims of Jews and Arabs to Palestine, we regard it as essential that a clear statement of the following principles should be made:

I. That Jew shall not dominate Arab and Arab shall not dominate Jew in Palestine. II. That Palestine shall be neither a Jewish state nor an Arab state. III. That the form of government ultimately to be established, shall, under international guarantees, fully protect and preserve the interests in the Holy Land of Christendom and of the Moslem and Jewish faiths.

Thus Palestine must ultimately become a state which guards the rights and interests of Moslems, Jews and Christians alike; and accords to the inhabitants, as a whole, the fullest measure of self-government, consistent with the three paramount principles set forth above. . . .

Recommendation No. 4. We have reached the conclusion that the hostility between Jews and Arabs and, in particular, the determination of each to achieve domination, if necessary by violence, make it almost certain that, now and for some time to come, any attempt to establish either an independent Palestinian State or independent Palestinian States would result in civil strife such as might threaten the peace of the world.

We therefore recommend that, until this hostility disappears, the Government of Palestine be continued as at present under mandate pending the execution of a trusteeship agreement under the United Nations. . . .

Recommendation No. 5. Looking towards a form of ultimate self-government, consistent with the three principles laid down in Recommendation No. 3, we recommend that the mandatory or trustee should proclaim the principle that Arab economic, educational and political advancement in Palestine is of equal importance with that of the Jews; and should at once prepare measures designed to bridge the gap which now exists and raise the Arab standard of living to that of the Jews; and so bring the two peoples to a full appreciation of their common interest and common destiny in the land where both belong. . . .

Recommendation No. 6. We recommend that, pending the early reference to the United Nations and the execution of a trusteeship agreement, the mandatory should administer Palestine according to the mandate which declares with regard to immigration that "The administration of Palestine, while ensuring that the rights and position of other sections of the population are not prejudiced, shall facilitate Jewish immigration under suitable conditions." . . .

Recommendation No. 7. (a) We recommend that the Land Transfers Regulations of 1940 be rescinded and replaced by regulations based on a policy of freedom in the sale, lease or use of land, irrespective of race, community or creed, and providing adequate protection for the interests

of small owners and tenant cultivators; *(b)* We further recommend that steps be taken to render nugatory and to pro-
hibit provisions in conveyances, leases and agreements re-
lating to land which stipulate that only members of one
race, community or creed may be employed on or about or
in connection therewith; *(c)* We recommend that the Government should exercise such close supervision over the
Holy Places and localities such as the Sea of Galilee and its
vicinity as will protect them from desecration and from
uses which offend the conscience of religious people, and
that such laws as are required for this purpose be enacted
forthwith. . . .

Recommendation No. 8. Various plans for large-scale
agricultural and industrial development in Palestine have
been presented for our consideration; these projects, if successfully carried into effect, could not only greatly enlarge
the capacity of the country to support an increasing population but also raise the living standards of Jew and Arab
alike.

We are not in a position to assess the soundness of these
specific plans; but we cannot state too strongly that, however technically feasible they may be, they will fail unless
there is peace in Palestine. Moreover their full success re-
quires the willing cooperation of adjacent Arab states, since
they are not merely Palestinian projects. We recommend
therefore that the examination, discussion and execution
of these plans be conducted, from the start and throughout, in full consultation and cooperation not only with the
Jewish Agency but also with the governments of the neighboring Arab States directly affected. . . .

Recommendation No. 9. We recommend that, in the interests of the conciliation of the two peoples and of general
improvement of the Arab standard of living, the educa-

tional system of both Jews and Arabs be reformed, including the introduction of compulsory education within a reasonable time. . . .

Recommendation No. 10. We recommend that, if this Report is adopted, it should be made clear beyond all doubt to both Jews and Arabs that any attempt from either side, by threats of violence, by terrorism, or by the organization or use of illegal armies to prevent its execution, will be resolutely suppressed.

Furthermore, we express the view that the Jewish Agency should at once resume active cooperation with the Mandatory in the suppression of terrorism and of illegal immigration, and in the maintenance of that law and order throughout Palestine which is essential for the good of all, including the new immigrants. . . .

United Nations Resolution on the Partition of Palestine, 29 November 1947

(See Map 5, p. 128.)

Plan of Partition with Economic Union

PART I. FUTURE CONSTITUTION AND
GOVERNMENT OF PALESTINE

A. TERMINATION OF MANDATE,
PARTITION AND INDEPENDENCE

1. The Mandate for Palestine shall terminate as soon as possible but in any case not later than 1 August 1948.

2. The armed forces of the mandatory Power shall be progressively withdrawn from Palestine, the withdrawal to be completed as soon as possible but in any case not later than 1 August 1948.

The mandatory Power shall advise the Commission as far in advance as possible, of its intention to terminate the Mandate and to evacuate each area.

The mandatory Power shall use its best endeavours to ensure that an area situated in the territory of the Jewish State, including a seaport and hinterland adequate to provide facilities for a substantial immigration, shall be evacuated at the earliest possible date and in any event not later than 1 February 1948.

3. Independent Arab and Jewish States and the Special International Regime for the City of Jerusalem, set forth in part III of this plan, shall come into existence in Palestine two months after the evacuation of the armed forces of the mandatory Power has been completed but in any case not later than 1 October 1948. The boundaries of the Arab State, the Jewish State, and the City of Jerusalem shall be as described in parts II and III below.

4. The period between the adoption by the General Assembly of its recommendation on the question of Palestine and the establishment of the independence of the Arab and Jewish States shall be a transitional period.

Glossary

aliya	Immigration wave; literally, "going up" to Palestine.
al-Salaf	The pious forerunners of Islam; the community of Elders.
effendi	Member of the Arab landowning class.
fatwa	Islamic religious edict.
Hagana	Clandestine military arm of the Jewish Agency.
Haskalah	Jewish Enlightenment, or spiritual liberation.
Histadrut	Central labor union of the Jewish community.
Irgun	Hebrew, "Organization"; short form of Irgun Zwai Leumi, "National Military Organization."
jihad	Islamic Holy War.
Lehi	Abbreviated form of Lohamei Herut Israel, "Israel Freedom Fighters."

mufti	Muslim jurisconsult qualified to issue religious edicts on religious questions.
saison	French, "hunting season"; the Jewish community's campaign against its own dissidents (1944–1945).
Sanhedrin	Ancient Jewish rabbinical assembly.
Shariʿa	The revealed Holy Law of Islam.
sharif	Ruler of the Muslim holy cities Mecca and Medina.
ulama	Class of religious scholars, jurists, teachers, and dignitaries; the nearest Islamic approximation to a priesthood.
vilayet	Turkish adaptation of Arabic *wilāyah*, "administrative district."
wali	Turkish provincial governor.
Waqf	Land endowed for religious purposes.
Yishuv	The Jewish community in mandatory Palestine.

Suggested Reading

(English-language sources only)

Chapter One

On the development of Arab nationalism since the nineteenth century, see George Antonius's classic, *The Arab Awakening* (London, 1938); as well as Sylvia G. Haim, *Arab Nationalism: An Anthology* (Berkeley and Los Angeles, 1962); Albert Hourani, *Arabic Thought in the Liberal Age, 1798–1939* (Oxford, 1962); Hisham Sharabi, *Arab Intellectuals and the West* (Baltimore, 1970); and Bernard Lewis, *The Middle East and the West* (Bloomington, Ind., 1964).

For studies of the Middle East during World War I, see Elie Kedourie, *England and the Middle East* (London, 1956); Aaron Klieman, *The Cairo Conference: The Foundations of British Policy in the Arab World* (Baltimore, 1970); and Howard Sachar, *The Emergence of the Middle East* (London, 1974).

For the debate on the Husayn-McMahon correspondence, see Antonius, *The Arab Awakening;* and Elie Kedourie, *In the Anglo-Arab Labyrinth* (Cambridge, 1976).

See also Isaiah Friedman, "The McMahon-Hussein Correspondence and the Question of Palestine," *Journal of
Contemporary History* 5, no. 2 (1970):83–122; "The
McMahon-Hussein Correspondence: Comments by Ar-
nold Toynbee and a Reply by Isaiah Friedman," *Journal
of Contemporary History* 5, no. 4 (1970):185–201; and
Abdul Latif Tibawi, *Anglo-Arab Relations and the Palestine Question, 1914–1921* (London, 1977).

Chapter Two

Works on the history of the Zionist movement include
Ben Halpern, *The Idea of the Jewish State* (Cambridge,
Mass., 1969); Arthur Hertzberg, *The Zionist Idea* (New
York, 1972); Walter Z. Laqueur, *A History of Zionism*
(London, 1972); and David Vital, *The Origins of Zionism*
(Oxford, 1975).

For history and interpretations of the Balfour Decla-
ration, see Isaiah Friedman, *The Question of Palestine,
1914–1918* (London, 1973); Leonard Stein, *The Balfour
Declaration* (London, 1961); Barbara Tuchman, *The Bible
and the Sword: England and Palestine from the Bronze
Age to Balfour* (New York, 1956); and Meyer Vereté, "The
Origins of the Balfour Declaration," *Middle Eastern Stud-
ies* 6 (January 1970):48–76. For a "revisionist" view of
Churchill's role in Jewish questions, see Michael J. Cohen,
Churchill and the Jews (London, 1985).

Chapter Three

There are three general histories of the Palestine mandate:
ESCO Foundation for Palestine, Inc., *Palestine: A Study of
the Jewish, Arab, and British Policies* (New Haven, Conn.,

1947); Jacob Coleman Hurewitz, *The Struggle for Palestine* (New York, 1950); and Christopher Sykes, *Crossroads to Israel* (London, 1965; Bloomington, Ind., 1973).

On initial problems and community relations, see Neil Caplan, *Palestine Jewry and the Arab Question* (London, 1978); and Bernard Wasserstein, *The British in Palestine: The Mandatory Government and the Arab-Jewish Conflict, 1917–1929* (London, 1979). On the Zionists' economic problems and immigration policy, see Moshe Mossek, *The Immigration Policy of Sir Herbert Samuel* (London, 1979); and Samuel N. Eisenstadt, *Israeli Society* (London, 1967). For a highly tendentious polemic on the demography of Palestine over the past century, see Joan Peters, *From Time Immemorial: The Origins of the Arab-Jewish Conflict over Palestine* (New York, 1984). For an "inside" view of a Zionist leader's perception of the Arab problem, see Shabtai Teveth, *Ben-Gurion and the Palestinian Arabs* (Oxford, 1985).

An authoritative, and perhaps the definitive, history of Palestinian Arab nationalism is Yehoshua Porat's *The Emergence of the Palestinian-Arab National Movement*, vol. 1: *1918–1929*, vol. 2: *1929–1939* (London, 1974, 1977). For the political system of the Jewish community, see David Horowitz and Moshe Lissak, *Origins of the Israeli Polity* (Chicago, 1978); and Yonatan Shapiro, *The Formative Years of the Israeli Labour Party* (London, 1976).

Political and social changes from the 1930s on are discussed in Michael J. Cohen, *Palestine: Retreat from the Mandate, 1936–1945* (New York, 1978); John Marlowe, *The Seat of Pilate* (London, 1959); Yehuda Bauer, *From Diplomacy to Resistance: A History of Jewish Palestine, 1939–1945* (Philadelphia, 1970); and Joel S. Migdal, ed., *Palestinian Society and Politics* (Princeton, N.J., 1980). On the political ramifications of land sales by Arabs to Jews, see Kenneth W. Stein, *The Land Question in Palestine, 1917–1939* (Chapel Hill, N.C., 1984). For the implications of the Holocaust, see Bernard Wasserstein, *Britain and the Jews of Europe, 1939–1945* (Oxford, 1979).

Chapter Four

For comprehensive diplomatic surveys, see Michael J. Cohen, *Palestine and the Great Powers, 1945–1948* (Princeton, N.J., 1982); Elizabeth Monroe, "Mr. Bevin's 'Arab' Policy," *St. Antony's Papers*, no. 11, *Middle East*, no. 2; and Nicolas Bethell, *The Palestine Triangle* (London, 1979). Two recently published studies that have respectively placed the British Labour government's Palestine policies in their global and regional contexts are Sir Alan Bullock's *Ernest Bevin: Foreign Secretary* (London, 1983); and William Roger Louis's *The British Empire in the Middle East, 1945–1951* (Oxford, 1984).

For American policy, see Clark Clifford, "Factors Influencing President Truman's Decision to Support Partition and Recognize the State of Israel," in *Israel in the Evolution of American Foreign Policy* (New York, 1978); Robert J. Donovan, *Conflict and Crisis: The Presidency of Harry S. Truman, 1945–1948* (New York, 1977); Zvi Ganin, *Truman, American Jewry, and Israel* (New York, 1979); John Snetsinger, *Truman, the Jewish Vote, and the Creation of Israel* (Stanford, Calif., 1974); and Evan Wilson, *Decision on Palestine* (Stanford, Calif., 1979).

Soviet policy toward Zionism and the state of Israel is discussed in Yaacov Roi, *Soviet Decision Making in Practice: The USSR and Israel, 1947–1954* (New Brunswick, N.J., 1980).

Descriptions of the Jews' rebellion against British rule are found in Menahem Begin, *The Revolt* (Tel Aviv, 1951); and John Bowyer-Bell, *Terror out of Zion* (New York, 1977). On Israel's strategy during the War of Independence, see Netanel Lorch, *Israel's War of Independence* (Jerusalem, 1968).

On Arab policy, see Fred Khouri, *The Arab-Israeli Dilemma* (New York, 1968); *King 'Abdallah of Jordan: My Memoirs Completed*, translated from the Arabic by Harold W. Glidden (Washington, D.C., 1954); and Musa al-Alami, "The Lesson of Palestine," *Middle East Journal* 3 (October 1949): 373–405.

Index

tions with Morgenthau, 47; replaced by Ben-Gurion as Zionist leader, 99
Welt, Die, 36
West, Islamic rejection of, 4–5
"Westerners," in British World War I policy making, 15
Wilson, Sir Henry, 61
Wilson, Woodrow: draft of Balfour Declaration submitted to, 52; Jews as advisers to, 47; and "mandate" terminology, 63–64; and principle of self-rule, 26; war aims of, and British policy toward Middle East, 45–46
World War I, 97; Arab nationalist movement on eve of, 8–9; effect of, on Jewish settlements in Palestine, 40–41; role of Arab military revolt in, 26–28. *See also* Great Britain
World War II, 95–105

Yishuv, 79; demographic problems of, 89–90, 99; ends allegiance to Britain after 1939 white paper, 93, 96; governmental revenue generated by, 73–74; and Jewish terror, 104; and lessons drawn from 1936 Arab revolt, 93; response of, to partition vote, 127
Young Christians, 4

Zionists, and Zionist movement, 9, 23, 30–31, 40–41; Ben-Gurion succeeds Weizmann as leader of, 99; and Biltmore Programme, 98–99; British negotiations with, 41–42, 45–54; English Jewry hostile to, 50–52; First Congress of, 36; and Jewish terrorism, 104–105, 122, 123; land purchases by, in Palestine, 73–78; in lobby effort to secure partition, 126–127; and mandate, 78–83; and policy of immigration to Palestine, 108–109; rebellion of, 112–117; and rejection of Morrison-Grady plan, 111–112; Sixteenth Congress of, 84–85; Sixth Congress of, 37, 38; socialist, 37; "Spiritual," 38; split among, over Jewish Division, 98–99. *See also* Political Zionism